MW01223999

The Teachable Journey:
(How to Quit Making the Same Mistakes and Open Your Doors of Possibility)

Rob & Katie —
Thanks for all the
lessons you have taught to
Loutta & I through your lives
Stay Teachable!
Cal Habig

Calvin Habig

Pacesetter Publishing

Unless otherwise noted, all scripture is quoted from the *The New International Version*. (2011). Grand Rapids, MI: Zondervan.

Pacesetter Publishing

12899 SW Bradley Lane

Portland, OR 97224

ISBN-13: 978-1503302914
ISBN-10: 1503302911

CONTENTS

ACKNOWLEDGEMENTS

This book, which I thought would be a several month project, has now extended out for over five years. There have been times of dryness, times of inspiration, times of self-doubt, times of frantic writing and times of confusion. My wife is credited in the book with beginning me on this journey, but her persistent encouragement has also allowed me to complete it. I deeply appreciate the work that my eldest son, Ryan Habig did on helping take my vision for a cover and use his graphic arts skills to bring it to reality. My OHSU Men's Cancer Writing Group, especially Ryan V. have been a constant inspiration through much of that time and while not directly involved in the book's content development, have continually encouraged me to stay true to my voice. Many people have contributed to my thinking through encouragement, conversations, Facebook posts and reviewing the manuscript. That latter category includes Blake W., Bob M., Heather K., Loretta H., and Vibeke K. all of whose input I deeply appreciate. Any errors that remain are totally my own.

Fable: The Scotty Who Knew Too Much
(adapted from James Thurber)

Several summers ago there was a Scotty dog who went to the country for a visit. He decided that all the farm dogs were cowards because they were afraid of a certain animal that had a white stripe down its back.

"You are a wimp and I can beat you up!" the Scotty said to the farm dog who lived in the house where the Scotty was visiting. "I certainly can beat up the animal with the white stripe too. Show him to me."

"Don't you want to ask any questions about him?" said the farm dog.

"Nah," said the Scotty. "You ask the questions."

So the farm dog took the Scotty into the woods and showed him the white-striped animal, and the Scotty closed in on him, growling and slashing. It was all over in a moment, and the Scotty lay on his back.

When he came to, the farm dog asked, mockingly, "What happened?"

"He threw acid," said the Scotty, "but he never laid a glove on me."

A few days later the farm dog told the Scotty there was another animal all the farm dogs were afraid of.

"Lead me to him," said the Scotty. "I can beat anything that doesn't wear horseshoes."

"Don't you want to ask any questions about him?" said the farm dog.

"Nah," said the Scotty. "Just show me where he hangs out." So the farm dog led him to a place in the woods and pointed out the little animal when he came along.

"The clown," said the Scotty. "A pushover." He closed in, leading with his left and exhibiting some mighty fancy footwork. In less than a second, the Scotty was flat on his back, and when he woke up the farm dog was pulling quills out of him and laughing.

"What happened?" asked the farm dog sarcastically.

"He pulled a knife on me," said the Scotty. "But at least I've learned how you fight up here in the country, and now because you have made jest of me, I know I can beat you up, and so I will!"

So he closed in on the farm dog, holding his nose with one front paw to ward off the acid and covering his eyes with the other front paw to keep out the knives. The Scotty couldn't see his opponent, and he couldn't smell his opponent, and he was so badly beaten that he had to be taken back to the city and put in a nursing home.

Moral? It is better to ask some of the questions than to know all the answers.

(updated from James Thurber, Fables For Our Time–III
The New Yorker, February 18, 1939 p. 19)

CHAPTER 1: THE QUESTION I COULDN'T ANSWER

It was the question for which I didn't have an answer.

My wife and I were talking about the fact that six months had passed since I had been laid off from my job. No reasons had been given for my termination after nine years of employment. Just: "You're done." The very same week my doctor had told me that I had fast-growing prostate cancer. Now we were six months since I had left my job and three months past my cancer surgery. My severance pay was coming to an end and there were no prospects for a new job on the horizon.

We had made several decisions:
1.   We did not want to move away from Portland, or at least from the Pacific Northwest. The "Great Recession" was just getting started and it was a lousy time to sell a house. Both of our sons had married girls from the Pacific Northwest and our first grandchild had just been born.
2.   I was going to take a break from my profession of 30 years.
3.   I was working to expand my online college teaching.

But those were external workings. My wife was just as (or more) concerned with internal workings. So she asked the question for which I had no answer:

"So what has God taught you in this past six months?"

As a man who had accepted Christ over forty years ago and who had taught the Bible and the Christian walk for decades, unfortunately I had to answer:

"I don't know…nothing as far as I could see."

She looked at me with that puzzled, "Don't you think that's strange," kind of look and the conversation moved on.

But I honestly didn't know what, if anything, God was trying to teach me.

The question was especially poignant because we had just returned from a visit to our son and his wife's home in the Seattle area. (Actually, if the truth be told, we had gone up to see our newborn granddaughter!)

We had worshipped with Ryan and Michelle and the church where Ryan served as worship pastor.

The preacher at their congregation had been preaching on Psalm 42 and 43: "Knowing God's Presence in the Face of Suffering."

God had used Ryan's preacher to drive home two points loud and clear:
- Suffering can teach, but
- Suffering only teaches the teachable.

And then that week my wife asked her fateful question.

The question haunted me. I had experienced one of the most traumatic events in my life; I had had half a year to think and pray about it. Although I believe that God had spoken to me in a number of important ways, I couldn't say that he had TAUGHT me anything out of this specific situation.

I had taught in the area of God's will for many years. I had read many books on God's will.

But this was different from the general subject of knowing God's will. This had just as much to do with ME as it did with God.

If God was speaking, was I listening?

And if I said that I was listening, was I actually ready to "hear" and act upon what God had said?

That got me thinking about teachableness. Was I teachable? Since teachableness is an attitude, did I have an attitude of being teachable or a teachable spirit? (I use these terms synonymously).

For years I had taught the old maxim that in leadership recruitment and development we needed F.A.T. people. Not necessarily people of girth, but people who were

- Faithful
- Available
- Teachable

But what were the implications of #3: teachable?

For years I had also heard "God wastes no experience in our lives," and I believed it. Not that God directly causes everything that happens to us, but God "uses" or "transforms" every experience.

If I was NOT teachable, why not? Were there blocks that kept me from being teachable (if I truly was)? Were there things I could do, attitudes I could develop, to remove those possible barriers? Similarly, were there things I could do and attitudes I could develop that would put me in a better place to be teachable?

The definition of teachable isn't that difficult. *The American Heritage Dictionary* defines teachable as "That can be taught (teachable skills); able and willing to learn (teachable youngsters)".[1]

I knew what the word meant.[2] That wasn't the question. The question was, "Was I teachable? Was I able and willing to learn?"

My normal course of action when faced with dilemmas is to go to God's Word. A quick word search revealed that the word "teachable" is not found in the Bible (with one possible exception regarding church leadership, but we'll get to that later).

There were EXAMPLES of teachableness in the Bible. There were examples of people having a LACK of teachableness. The book of Proverbs is FILLED with axioms about the importance of being teachable. But the exact word is not used.

One of my favorite Christian authors, Gordon McDonald called teachability one of the most important characteristics of a disciple: "Without the trait of teachability, a disciple is not a complete disciple."[3]

Well, that's a pretty big statement for a word that isn't even used in the Bible!

And so I launched on a quest. But at that point, six months after being asked to resign, I had no idea about the journey that I was taking. Little did I know that the real (and harder) lessons were still to come….

Chapter One: Questions for Personal Thought and Group Discussion

- Have you ever been confronted with a time in your life when you realized you were not teachable? What did you do with that realization?

- Do you have someone in your life who will confront you (lovingly) if you have a lack of teachableness? Who is that? Are you willing to give them permission to do so?

- How would you describe the relationship between knowing the will of God and being teachable?

- How has pain made you more teachable? Less teachable?

- What was your reaction to the statement "God wastes no experience in our lives"?

- What was your reaction to Gordon McDonald's quote, "Without the trait of teachability, a disciple is not a complete disciple"?

Fable #2: The Chickens and the Fox

Every morning mama chicken would warn her chicks about the fox. "The fox is clever and loves to eat little chickens. Beware!" Each night she would quiz her babies, "What did mother tell you this morning?" And they would faithfully reply, "The fox is clever and loves to eat little chickens. Beware!"

One day as the chicks were out exploring they saw a beautiful red fox come slinking out of the forest. "Oh, his fur looks so soft, I want to touch it!" said one. "His face has such a smile, I want to get to know him" said another. "I can see his eyes," said a third. "He looks so clever. I have a question I want to ask him."

At just that moment the mother hen saw the fox and let out a cry of defense. The chicks quickly fled and barely escaped with their lives.

Moral: To have identified a lesson is not necessarily to have learned it.

CHAPTER 2: WHAT IS A TEACHABLE SPIRIT?

To hold the same views at forty as we held at twenty is to have been stupefied for a score of years, and take rank, not as a prophet, but as a non-teachable brat, well birched [punished] and none the wiser.

-- Robert Louis Stevenson

So if this characteristic of teachability is so important, we would be wise (it would seem) to understand as specifically as possible how to define it.

Ryan J. Bell is an intelligent man. He describes himself as a "Speaker, Author, Teacher, Activist."[4] He was Adjunct Professor in the Doctor of Ministry program at Fuller Theological Seminary and the Global Studies Department at Azusa Pacific University.

He was also, for many years, a minister in the Seventh Day Adventist denomination. He contributed significantly to his denomination and was awarded an Innovative Church of the Year award from the North American Division of his church. He also advocated vocally for a change in the church's position on a number of progressive issues. He states,

> I had been an outspoken critic of the church's approach to our gay, lesbian, bisexual and transgendered members--that approach being exclusion or, at best, second class membership ("we won't kick you out but you can't participate in leadership"). Through the years, I had also been a critic of the church's treatment of women, their approach to evangelism and their tunnel-vision approach to church growth.[5]

In early 2013, Bell was asked to resign as a pastor from his denomination. For the rest of 2013 he struggled with what faith meant for him. He couldn't make himself read the Bible, pray, or even attend church regularly.

So, with the dawning of 2014, he declared that he was going to "try on" atheism for a year. He declared,

> For the next 12 months I will live as if there is no God. I will not pray, read the Bible for inspiration, refer to God as the cause of things or hope that God might intervene and change my own or someone else's circumstances....I will read atheist "sacred texts"--from Hobbes and Spinoza to Russell and Nietzsche to the trinity of New Atheists, Hitchens, Dawkins and Dennett. I will explore the various ways of being atheist, from naturalism (Voltaire, Dewey, et al) to the new 'religious atheists' (Alain de Botton and Ronald Dworkin). I will also attempt to speak to as many actual atheists as possible--scholars, writers and ordinary unbelievers--to learn how they have come to their non-faith and what it means to them. I will visit atheist gatherings and try it on.[6]

Bell states that he does this in the name of pursuing truth. He desires to be "teachable".

Is that an image of what it means to be teachable?   Reacting emotionally to what has been a great deal of hurt? Filling one's mind with only one way of thinking, ignoring the alternative view? Is that what being teachable is, whether that "content" is atheist or Christian or something else?

How do you define words like "teachable"? It is a common enough word, but when we actually begin to delve into it, we often bring our own baggage to how we define words.

I teach an eastern religions class for the online department of a national university and in the first week of the class, I ask my students to answer and discuss the following:

Without using a resource, define the following terms in your own words:

- Religion
- Sacred
- Myth
- god (lower case "g", not upper case "G")
- Ritual

Almost every student who takes the class comments on what a surprise answering this question becomes. These terms are ones that we just presume that we know, and that everyone else understands these terms as meaning the same thing that I do.

The first surprise for the students is when they actually try to put what they believe these terms mean into words. It is much harder for most than they first thought. Once they have done that and enter into the online discussions about their and everyone else's definitions, they realize that not only is their definition often incomplete, but also other people have very different definitions from their own!   It is a credit to my students that I have seldom had any angry discussions on these definitions, but there have definitely been disagreements!

It is the same with the term "teachable." If I were to ask 100 people what it means, and then to explain it, while the definitions may be similar, the explanations would vary wildly.

I've already given the definition of "teachable" from the *American Heritage Dictionary*. Another of those ultimate authorities on all things linguistic, dictionary.com defines "teachable" as "capable of being instructed".[7] It does not define the realm of that capability (mentally capable? attitudinally capable? volitionally capable?). *The Free Dictionary* goes a step further in its definition: "Able and willing to learn."[8]   Here we see the divisions that I wondered about earlier: mental capability and attitudinal capability. While the edition of the *Oxford English Dictionary* I consulted did not have "teachable," it did have: 1. "teach: impart knowledge to or instruct (someone) in how to do something, especially in a school or as part of a recognized programme. 2. Give instruction in (a subject or skill). 3. Cause to learn by example of experience."[9]

The twentieth century educator and author Steven Covey defined teachableness as "operating with the assumption that you do not have all the answers, all the insights, and valuing the different viewpoints, judgment, and experiences followers may have."[10]

We might rework all that to get an acceptable definition of teachable: 1. able to receive "knowledge or to be instructed in how to do something." 2. To be able to receive instruction in (a subject or skill). 3. To learn by example or experience.

The three parts of the definition are definitely related. The ability of being "able to receive knowledge" probably includes not only the ability, but the willingness to learn. To be teachable implies the ability to learn. A chair cannot be "teachable." A tree, though living, cannot be "teachable". (It can be "trained" to grow in a specific direction or manner, but it has not been "taught." It has been directed contrary to what is its natural will.) It may be debated whether a computer can be "taught". I would suggest not, but it is a distraction from my point to go down that road.

Being teachable is a product of reasoned thought and independent-decision making that is reserved for mammals of higher abilities.

Most of us recognize that the longer we live, the less teachable we seem to become. The Bible stresses that teachableness is a characteristic of small children. While the Bible does not specifically STATE this, the commentators are pretty unanimous in agreeing that this is the implication of such verses as:

Matt. 11:25: *At that time Jesus said, "I praise you, Father, Lord of heaven and earth, because you have hidden these things from the wise and learned, and revealed them to little children.*

Matt. 18:2-3: *He called a little child, whom he placed among them. And he said: "Truly I tell you, unless you change and become like little children, you will never enter the kingdom of heaven.*

Mark 10:15: *Truly I tell you, anyone who will not receive the kingdom of God like a little child will never enter it."*

Jesus says that we should mimic (or follow the example) of small children in this regard.

What Teachableness is Not

We cannot adequate define something by simply describing what it is not. However, if we take the definition suggested above, it can be helpful to place it in contrast to some other ideas that are sometimes confused for being teachable. This enables us to refine the above definition a bit more closely.

1.   We might get the impression that teachableness is **a passive thing.** I believe that is incorrect. Teachableness is an active thing. At a minimum, teachableness is an act of the will. The books of Psalms and Proverbs speak of the stubbornness of the mule and donkey.

Do not be like the horse or the mule,
which have no understanding
but must be controlled by bit and bridle
or they will not come to you. (Ps 32:9)

A whip for the horse, a bridle for the donkey,
and a rod for the backs of fools! (Prov. 26:3)

For millennia, most have recognized the nature of mules and donkeys. The ancient Greek writers Homer and Aesop labeled donkeys as "stupid, servile and stubborn".[11] We are to choose (an act of the will) to not be like the donkey, stubborn and unteachable (cf. Prov. 26:3).

2.   **Teachableness is not, however, gullibility.**

I don't like to think of myself as gullible person. I like to think of myself as a logical person who expects evidence for claims of fact. The reality is that in many things I usually think critically. But when it comes to interpersonal relations, it seems I can be horribly gullible.

As I was writing this section, my wife made the comment that I am "a sucker for sad cases." I reacted strongly to that accusation. "No way! Give me an example!"

I finally asked her to stop after she had named example after example. She was right.

My gullibility is not so much a matter of intellect, but of relationships. Show me an intellectual argument and I can usually point out the logical fallacies very quickly, but when it comes to believing in people, I will believe the most unreasonable things.

Early on in my career, I was a soft touch for the transients and panhandlers that hit on every church. I believed the most incredible stories that people told me.

I wanted to believe that others' motives were as good as mine (or at least the motives I wanted to attribute to myself!).

One time a woman came by the church and said that her children hadn't eaten in several days. She (of course) wanted money for food. Fortunately church policy did not allow me to give out cash, but we had a credit account at a nearby restaurant. I gave the lady directions and told her I would call the restaurant to expect them. In walking her out (which she kept saying was totally unnecessary), I stepped outside the church building. Fortunately for me (unfortunately for her) she had parked right in front of the church. There, her (unmentioned) husband sat in a station wagon laden down with groceries from (I presume) visits to other churches. I was crushed to be lied to in such a bald-faced way.

The story repeated itself enough times that I (unfortunately) began to be cynical of even legitimate needs.

But even more than **believing** people, I was extremely gullible when it came to believing in people. There has been a whole host of individuals for whom the evidence pointed that they either were misrepresenting a situation or themselves or had much less potential than I wanted to believe that they had.

It was not just transients I believed.

One of my lifelong strengths is to see the potential in people and see what God could do through them and then try to equip them to live up to that potential. A number of staff persons, counselees, church leaders and community peers picked that up and (with my encouragement and suggestions) grew even beyond where even I believed that they could grow!

There were, however, staff persons, counselees, church leaders and community peers whom I believed had more potential than they had demonstrated. This was the dark side of one of my strengths. I saw more potential in many of them than was likely there. I have spent countless hours and hundreds of dollars on fellow believers who I was POSITIVE could be a success and a benefit to the kingdom of God if only they had the one chance that I could give to them. I suspect it has to do with projecting my own needs onto them.

But many did not. Perhaps it was bad habits or bad attitudes, but whatever, they refused to live up to the potential that (I believed) was in them. The way I saw them was not necessarily the way they saw themselves. Groups of leaders in churches and community organizations have said over and over that they were going to do something, only to show in the end that they really had no intention of doing what they said.

The problem, however, was not just my disappointment. I would pour hours and hours of time and financial resources to give them opportunities. In the process I have lost a lot of money, bailed friends out of jail, gone contrary to what my experience and intuition told me I should do, foregone opportunities to build my own business to help others build theirs, even had a pistol pulled on me and pointed to my face (because I "knew" of the potential of the person holding the gun).

Whether it is real or not, there is a common perception that Christian people are generally gullible.

In February 1993, the *Washington Post* published a now-infamous article which described evangelical Christians as "largely poor, uneducated and easy to control."

That image of Christian gullibility continues to crop up regularly to this day. In 2005, the CEO of HealthSouth, Richard Scrushy, was accused of financial fraud (after 5 of his associates pled guilty and pointed to him as the instigator of the conspiracy) and of pocketing $300 million. As soon as the charges were filed, Scrushy left his suburban white church and (according to ANOTHER *Washington Post* feature article),

"joined a predominantly black congregation in a blue-collar neighborhood. He bought a half-hour of local TV for a morning prayer show featuring himself and his wife, and frequent guest spots by black ministers. He had a prayer group praying for him every day at the trial. All this was in Birmingham, Ala., where HealthSouth was located and where the trial occurred."[12]

The clear implication of the article is that Scrushy was successful in manipulating the Christian people of Birmingham who (as the article labels them) were "poor, uneducated and easily led".

Does the Christian slant on the trait of teachableness include being gullible? What does it mean to be gullible? In his work, *Annals of Gullibility*, Stephen Greenspan (no sympathizer for Christian evangelicals) defines "gullibility" as "an unusual tendency toward being duped or taken advantage of."[13]

Another source (dictionary.com) defines gullible as: "easily deceived or cheated." It lists its synonyms as: "credulous, trusting, naive, innocent, simple, green."[14]

Greenspan notes four elements in gullibility: Situations + Cognition + Personality + State:

1. **Situation**: the con man may be very convincing or (better yet) use those around the victim to vouch for the integrity of the one doing the con.
2. **Cognition**: not using one's intelligence. Greenspan stresses that gullibility is NOT a matter of intelligence. Very intelligent people can be gullible. It is that they are not USING their intelligence. Perhaps the victim is bad at reading people or naïve about the type of investment covered by the scam (like uneducated in an area, lazy thinking, etc.).
3. **Personality**: perhaps they are unusually trusting or have a problem saying "no."
4. **State**:-the current physical or emotional state of the victim. Perhaps there is exhaustion, inebriation, infatuated with the con man, etc.)[15]

So does this describe the Christian of teachableness? Of course not. Greenspan (who also sees religious people as especially gullible) give the biblical examples of Samson (whom Greenspan labels, "the prototype of the dumb jock"), Eve and the Serpent, Lot being "raped" by his daughters, Jacob tricking both Esau out of his inheritance and Isaac out of his blessing, and Jacob being tricked by Laban into marrying Leah instead of Rachel.

But what Greenspan misses (I believe) is that these are never depicted in scripture as admirable actions or (especially not) actions to emulate. They are there are warnings of the foolishness of being gullible.

Greenspan describes "gullibility" as knowledge or wisdom unapplied. He contrasts it to trust, quoting the words of Julian Rotter that gullibility "is a foolish or naïve application of trust in situations where the warning signs are fairly evident."[16]

This would be right in line with what the Bible teaches. Gullibility is not the same as teachability and is not a positive Christian characteristic (no matter how common it may be among Christian people).

Proverbs 14:15 states: *"The simple believe anything, but the prudent give thought to their steps."*

Proverbs 15:32-33: *"Those who ignore instruction despise themselves, but those who heed admonition gain understanding. The fear of the LORD is instruction in wisdom, and humility goes before honor."*

Jesus seemed particularly concerned that his followers not be gullible. Listen to the drumbeat of his warnings in the following verses:

- Matt 24.4: *"Jesus answered: 'Watch out that no one deceives you.'"*

- Mark 8.15: *"Be careful," Jesus warned them. "Watch out for the yeast of the Pharisees and that of Herod."*

- Mark 12.38: *"As he taught, Jesus said, "Watch out for the teachers of the law. They like to walk around in flowing robes and be greeted with respect in the marketplaces…."*

- Mark 13.23: *"So be on your guard; I have told you everything ahead of time."*[17]

- Luke 21.8: *"He replied: "Watch out that you are not deceived. For many will come in my name, claiming, 'I am he,' and, 'The time is near.' Do not follow them.'"*

The Greek word that is used in these passages (and 127 more times in the New Testament) is the word blepo. (βλέπω). Blepo "denotes sense perception, e.g., being able to see as distinct from blindness".[18] There is, however, another word in the New Testament specifically for the physical ability to see (horao-ὁράω). Blepo is different from horao in that it expresses "a more intent, earnest contemplation".[19] Christ calls for his disciples not to be gullible, but to be intent and give earnest contemplation.

3.   Teachableness is not only different from gullibility, but it is also different from **low self-esteem.** People with low self-esteem are usually easily impressionable, either because they doubt their own judgment, or because they want love, affection and approval from others

Instead of being connected to low self-esteem, scripture's instruction on being teachable, promotes a healthy view of self: Proverbs 15:32-33 exhorts: *"Those who ignore instruction despise themselves, but those who heed admonition gain understanding. The fear of the LORD is instruction in wisdom, and humility goes before honor."*

For example, many former members of religious cults react very negatively when they hear the words "be teachable." Either before joining the cult or immediately after, their sense of competence and self-worth have often been compromised or destroyed. The purpose of this is so that the cult leader can convince the new disciple to follow his or her way without question. It is usually done in the name of "being teachable." Many of them have been impressed by the religious leader and longed for the certainty that be or she brings and have, thereby, been sucked into destructive religious groups.

Understandably, when those who have come out of cults hear people asking them to "be teachable" their defenses go up. Scripture passages which seem to have very neutral connotations to most people, such as *"He who comes after me must first of all deny himself..."* or *"forget...what lies behind,"* now bring strong negative reactions, including confusion and resentment from the former cult member.[20]

Those who are teachable show that they believe that they are capable of making changes; they are capable of understanding; they are capable of growing.

Teachableness is incompatible with low self-esteem.

4.   Similarly, teachableness is not the same as **insecurity or unsureness.** The book of Proverbs inseparably links wisdom and teachableness.

Solomon writes

Like a lame man's legs, which hang useless,
is a proverb in the mouth of fools.
Like one who binds the stone in the sling
is one who gives honor to a fool.
Like a thorn that goes up into the hand of a drunkard
is a proverb in the mouth of fools. (Prov. 26:7-9)

An insecure person or an unsure person will not know what to do with wisdom if he or she learns it. Insecurity leads to being protective of the status quo. It leads to wanting to keep things the same. The insecure or unsure person is not teachable because what they learn may require them to change, something that most insecure or unsure people are incapable of doing.

When I started at one of the churches I served I had come from a successful ministry in a county-seat type of rural church. I then moved to a larger suburban church. There were many differences (although not as many differences as people tried to convince me there were…people are still people, after all). Early on in that ministry at a staff meeting I made a suggestion about a particular program. One staff minister sneered and said, "Cal, we're not in (name of my former community). This is the city."

That staff person rang all of my insecurity bells. I was new. This was a long-time staff person. I recognized that things were different on the west coast from the Midwest and different from a county-seat type of church to a larger suburban church.

But while that staff person was wrong (both in attitude as well as in reality), my insecurity caused me to go defensive and to attempt to prove that I knew what I was talking about, to shut down what the staff person was saying instead of asking "What of this is valid and how can I learn from the comment and what of this person's comment do I need to just shrug off?"

My experience is that when I (or anyone else) am insecure, it shuts off one's ability to be teachable. When I am insecure, I am focusing on what others think and/or trying to build my own self-esteem. The result is that I am much less likely to face what I do not know, to admit what I cannot do, and to investigate what possibilities exist. I go into inward mode: either to convince myself that I am indeed sufficient unto myself, or to convince others that I know what I am talking about. To admit that I do not know something or do not have something under control (which is necessary for us to be teachable) is stifled when I am trying to convince myself or others of my worth and knowledge.

5.   To be teachable does not imply in any way that **there is no such thing as truth.** When someone is very dogmatic, there are those around him or her who tell them that they just "need to be teachable."

What is sometimes implied is that the dogmatic person shouldn't hold so strongly to his or her dogmatism because "there are many ways of looking at truth."

And there is a point at which that is true. None of us is the final repository of truth. None of us understand every aspect of every nuance of those things we know and believe. And so it IS important for us to be teachable: for us to be willing to adjust our dogmatism in light of new information and perspectives.

But that is not the same as moral relativism.

Moral relativism is rampant in our popular culture. "What's true for you is not necessarily true for me." It is rampant, I said, in our POPULAR culture. Not so in our intellectual culture. Philosophers understand that the statement "What's true for you is not necessarily true for me." is a self-defeating statement.

To say "What's true for you is not necessarily true for me" is to make an assertion of absolute truth: that what's true for you is not necessarily true for me. The fact that you can make the statement means that it isn't true.

In fact, teachability is quite the opposite: to say that something can be taught (and learned) means that certain things ARE true.

6.   Last, to be teachable does not mean simply **to have identified a lesson.** It means that we are eager (or at least willing) not simply to learn the lesson, but to actually implement it. As the chicks in our opening fable learned, identifying a lesson is not the same as learning the lesson.

It IS a step in the right direction to have identified the lesson. If I am self-deluded, or deluded by others, or deluded by sin, I may be oblivious to the fact that there is a lesson I need to learn. But circumstances (usually PAIN) can show me that I need to learn the lesson. For example, knowing that God wants me to lose weight is not the same as learning the lesson I need to learn about losing weight.

In Genesis 3, we have the sad example of Eve. Eve could (and even did) identify the lesson: *"We may eat fruit from the trees in the garden, but God did say, 'You must not eat fruit from the tree that is in the middle of the garden…or you will die.'"* But that does not mean that she was teachable: she obviously had not learned the lesson because she quickly fell to Satan's temptation.[21]

What are the characteristics of someone who identified a lesson but did not learn it? They would be able to verbalize the lesson. They might even be able to point it out in others, but they are not yet able to apply it to themselves. It would be identified as hypocrisy. Sadly, it is not a surprise to any of us that our knowledge exceeds our action. We are too often "knowledge rich" and "obedience poor". How do you identify a lesson? It could be from someone pointing it out to you. It could be from reading the Bible. It could be from observing the lives of others. The difference is that you don't apply it to yourself. Why don't you?

It could be that you think you are special and that the lesson does not apply to you. It could be that you are deluded by your sinful desires to believe that you know something, but which those same sinful desires keep you from being willing to apply. It could be that you are embarrassed by the mocking you may take from others because of the lesson's application. This would be the sin of fear of man. Is fear itself a sin? It might be when we are to trust in God. Definitely the fear of man is sin. What other fears can be considered a sin? Fearing God definitely is not. What was it that Eve feared? Perhaps nothing. Her sin was came from elsewhere.

Although Eve could identify the lesson—they were not to eat from the tree of knowledge of good and evil—still she was tempted to disobey the lesson which had been identified for her. Other factors came into play—doubting the goodness God's (He is not letting you be like him); doubting the Word of God (*"God has _not_ said…"*).

I wish I could say that I have no familiarity with this aspect of learning, but I do. Too many. I have known throughout ministry that my credibility doesn't come from degrees or even from experience, but from my character. That doesn't negate the importance of education or experience, but they are fairly useless without the character to validate and empower them.

But over time the temptation to let one boundary or another blur grew greater. "I deserve this exception," or "In the grand scheme, what does this boundary really matter?" or "Who really will know?"

But in each and every instance, whether or not the ethical stretch of the boundary was ever publicly known, I eventually saw that it weakened my spiritual power and usually bit me. I had to "learn" that lesson in a new (and usually harder) manner. And yet through all of that, if you had asked me where the source of my credibility and power in leadership came, I would state that it came from my character. I "knew" the lesson, but hadn't yet really learned it. Actually, I am probably still in process.

How does that apply in my life/our lives?

In many dance contests there is a dance called the limbo. It is a dance that came from the Caribbean island of Trinidad. Originally, the bar begins low and the dancer tries to dance under it without touching the ground with their hands. Each time he or she is successful, the bar is raised symbolizing emergence from death to life.

But in the westernized entertainment world (popularized by Julie Edwards and Chubby Checker, the bar begins high and each time the dancer is successful, the bar is lowered to provide a new challenge. In Chubby Checker's #2 Billboard hit "Limbo Rock" the singer sings:

Jack be limbo, Jack be quick
Jack go unda limbo stick
All around the limbo clock
Hey, let's do the limbo rock

Limbo lower now
Limbo lower now
How low can you go?[22]

In too many of our lives we push the boundaries of sin. Instead of "How LOW can you go?" it is "How FAR can you go without calling it sin?" The reality, however, is that the spirit of God says to flee from sin; to keep far from it.

Another example of identifying a lesson but not learning it is Judas. He was the treasurer of the group funds. When a woman came and anointed Jesus feet with perfume, he protested over the cost of the sacrifice, although there is no indication that the perfume was purchased out of the groups funds.

But one of his disciples, Judas Iscariot, who was later to betray him, objected, 'Why wasn't this perfume sold and the money given to the poor? It was worth a year's wages.' He did not say this because he cared about the poor but because he was a thief; as keeper of the money bag, he used to help himself to what was put into it. (John 12:4-6)

Judas claimed to be interested in the poor—he had identified a lesson (we should care for the poor) but we have no example of Judas doing anything about it and in fact in the one instance where he mentions it, scripture says that it was out of a motivation for greed and personal gain.

Each of us needs to ask ourselves, "So what lessons have I identified, but not yet learned?"

Stop.

Don't keep reading.

Before going on, think through that question for yourself: "So what lessons have I identified, but not yet learned?"

What will the lesson look like when/if it is learned? And is inconsistency always evidence that the lesson has not been learned?

It is not necessarily that one day you don't know it and the next you do. It seems logical that there are steps in learning a lesson. There is
- the level of identification.
- the level of seeing how to do something.
- the level of knowing how to do it.
- the level of practicing it with mistakes.
- the level of regularly incorporating it into your life.
- the level of mastery.

I see this demonstrated in the process of my grandchildren learning to walk. They can identify that other people walk upright on their feet. They see that others do it. They learn to stand upright, usually with an adult holding both hands, or while holding on to a table. There may be a few faltering attempts with falls.

But attempt after attempt usually increased the number of unaided steps taken. But it doesn't end there. In our home we have a sunken living room. One of our granddaughters Elli knew how to toddle on two feet pretty well. But when she came to the edge of the living room, this was a totally different story. Several times she tried to step out onto thin air and tumbled on her face instead. We backed up the learning a bit, and held her hand as she took the step down. After repeatedly doing it with help, Elli was able to take that step (haltingly at first) down into the living room. She had learned to walk, but there was another level: going down a step. Today (at age 3, she barely pauses when she comes to the drop-off, but steps down and moves on. She has mastered it.

Perhaps I should go back to the question of what will the lesson look like when it is learned? Or more accurately, what will my behavior look like when the lesson is learned? I don't know that total consistency is demanded, but it must be lived out in my life. It must be seen as the rule of practice in my life.

To be teachable does not mean to be gullible, passive, insecure, to have low self-esteem, to imply that nothing is, in fact, morally absolute or true, or to simply identify the lesson—but not learn it.

Look at the change in the character of Dorothy from the 1939 film "The Wizard of Oz". At the beginning of the movie, she is very unteachable.

When she tries to explain to her aunt and uncle and their hired hands how her dog Toto gets into villainous Miss Gulch's garden, one of the hired hands, Hunk offers a solution: "When you come home, don't go by Miss Gulch's place. Then Toto won't get in her garden, and you won't get in no trouble. See?"

Dorothy shrugs off the solution, "Oh Hunk…you just won't listen, that's all!"

Feeling brushed off by everyone around her, Dorothy runs away from home in order to save her dog Toto from the evil Miss Gulch.

As she wanders, she comes upon Professor Marvel, a mysterious travelling fortune-teller.

Even though his first two guesses at what she is doing are wrong, she is suddenly awed by Professor Marvel when he discerns (using more human psychology than divination) that she is running away from home and doing so because she is not appreciated at home. "They – they don't understand you at home. They don't appreciate you."

After entering into his fortune-tellers wagon, they sit down before his crystal ball ("the same genuine, magic, authentic crystal used by the Priests of Isis and Osiris in the days of the Pharaohs of Egypt in which Cleopatra first saw the approach of Julius Caesar and Marc Anthony, and so on, and so on.") He takes her basket from her, instructs her to close her eyes while he secretly rummages through her basket looking for clues about this young girl. Playing off of a picture in the basket of Dorothy and her Aunt Em, he describes situations derived from the picture. Finally, he describes Aunt Em collapsing on Dorothy's bed while clutching her heart. The gullible Dorothy Gale, believes that the Professor has truly seen through psychic powers and knows that she must rush back home to be with her aunt who misses her so much it may be killing her.

While Professor Marvel does good in convincing Dorothy to return to her home, he is only able to do it because this young girl is so gullible. Not teachable…gullible.

Contrast that with Dorothy at the end of the story. She and her compatriots, the supposedly brainless Scarecrow, heartless TinMan and cowardly Lion have destroyed the Wicked Witch of the West. But when they return to the Emerald City to claim their rewards: intelligence, compassion, bravery, and a magical trip back to Kansas, they discover that the Wizard is a fraud; a "humbug."

Right before Dorothy is shown by Glinda the Good Witch of the North, how to take herself back to Kansas, Glinda tells her that she couldn't send her back earlier because she "wouldn't have believed me. She had to learn it for herself."

The Tin Man asks, "What have you learned, Dorothy?"

"Well, I...I think that it...that it wasn't enough just to want to see Uncle Henry and Auntie Em...and it's that...if I ever go looking for my heart's desire again, I won't look any further than my own backyard. Because if it isn't there, I never really lost it to begin with!"

Dorothy had moved from stubborn unwillingness and gullibility, to become someone who is able to gain knowledge or to be instructed in how to do something, to be able to receive instruction in a subject or skill and to learn by example or experience.

She had become teachable.

Chapter Two: Questions for Personal Thought and Group Discussion

- How would you define the word "teachable"?

- What is it about small children that (usually) cause them to be teachable? Have you observed that "the longer we live, the less teachable many of us become"? If so, why do you think that is? Is it inevitable?

- Do you see Christians as especially gullible? Why or why not? How do you see gullibility as different from teachability?

- In what ways are you "knowledge rich" and "obedience poor"? (p. 21)

- What lessons have you identified, but not yet learned? How might you be able to identify AND learn them?

Fable #3 The Mouse Who Wanted to Fly

Once upon a time there was baby eagle who fell out of her nest. She fell quite a ways (since eagles nests are located so high) and was badly hurt. As she lay there, a small mouse came up and began to smell around to see if she was dead or alive. When he saw that the eaglet was alive, the mouse climbed on top of her and began squeaking as loud as he could, "Help! Help! Help!"

Soon the father eagle came and heard the cries for help. He swooped down, almost ready to eat the mouse, when he saw his injured daughter laying on the ground.

He helped care for his daughter until he was able to carry her back into the nest and was very thankful for the mouse's help. "If there is anything I can do for you", said the Father Eagle, "just name it and it shall be yours."

"Oh, I have watched you eagles fly for a long time and I have always wanted to fly. Could you carry me in your talons and let me fly beneath you?"

And so the Father Eagle consented. That flight was the first of many flights for the mouse. He and the eagle family became friends, and they even protected him when other eagles tried to eat him, because eagles love to eat tender little mice.

More and more the Father Eagle would bring the mouse back to the nest to check on how the daughter eaglet was recovering. They grew closer and closer and mouse and the father and daughter eagle began to feel like family towards one another.

Eventually the eaglet, now a small eagle had grown to the place where she was ready to fly. The daughter eagle teetered on the edge of the nest, afraid of again falling and being hurt. But Father Eagle kept nudging her until she toppled out of the nest. For a minute the eaglet struggled frantically, but quickly gained control of her wings and lifted herself up and began to fly. The Father Eagle, very proud of his daughter, flew out of the nest to show his daughter places she could now soar and see.

The little mouse was very proud that the eaglet he had helped to rescue was now able to fly. He thought, "I was not injured like the eaglet. If she has healed to the point that she could fly, I should be able to fly even better than her!"

The mouse stood on the edge of the nest, spread his scrawny arms and leapt, frantically beating his arms hoping they would allow him to soar.

When the father eagle came back and saw the dead carcass of his friend the mouse laying far beneath the eagles nest, he sadly told the moral to his daughter eagle:

Moral: "Lessons that one person may need to learn are not necessarily the lessons that others should learn."

Chapter 3: TEACHABLE ABOUT WHAT?

"The primary goal of education is to create people who are capable of doing new things, not simply of repeating what other generations have done —people who are creative, inventive and discoverers."

--Jean Piaget

This is the chapter that can't really be written. Perhaps as you looked through the table of contents, you saw this chapter and jumped right to it thinking, "I need to know what things I should be teachable about in order to start learning."

Sorry.

To make a list of lessons everyone needs to learn would be impossible. Think with me. If we take all of the people that have ever existed and multiply that by the number of lessons each individual needed to learn, it would be a staggering number.

Furthermore, there are lessons that others need to learn that I don't. A brain surgeon needs to learn certain lessons (If I need brain surgery, I definitely want him or her to have learned those lessons!) which are relatively useless to me.

While I believe that coaching skills can and should be learned by everyone because they are so useable in everyday life, realistically, there are lessons that I need to learn as an leadership coach that are really irrelevant to others.

To make a list of lessons everyone needs to learn would be impossible.

BUT...I believe there are categories of lessons. Those categories can be laid out in a matrix that I find helpful. The axes of the matrix are:

1. Who needs to learn it?

2. With what does it deal?

3. From whom does the lesson come?

Who Needs to Learn It.

LESSONS ALL PEOPLE MUST LEARN	LESSONS SPECIFIC GROUPS OF PEOPLE MUST LEARN	LESSONS SPECIFIC INDIVIDUALS MUST LEARN

As seen in the above diagram, there are three categories of lessons that need to be learned as it relates to the identity of the learner.

For example, there are **lessons that all people need to learn**. If they are mentally and physically capable, they need to learn to walk, to feed themselves, to speak the language of their culture, to earn an acceptable living in their culture, and to know how to interact with others in their society. These lessons are universal and there are many more.

Hebrews 11:6 says that there are even spiritual things that all people need to learn: *"anyone who comes to him must believe that he exists and that he rewards those who earnestly seek him."*

I Tim 2:3b-4 says, *"God our Savior...wants all people to be saved and to come to a knowledge of the truth."*

There are **lessons that specific groups of people need to learn.** I don't need to learn how to manage a canoe while fishing off a south Pacific island. I may want to experience it (I wouldn't hold my breath waiting, if I were you), but it is not something that I need to learn. And yet for many south Pacific islanders, that is a critical skill for them to learn in order to survive.

In the Old Testament, there were lessons that the nation of Israel specifically needed to learn. God wanted his people to be satisfied with Him as the king of Israel, administered by judges. But Israel clamored for a king. They wanted to be like other nations and have a king. *"But there shall be a king over us, that we also may be like all the nations, and that our king may judge us and go out before us and fight our battles."* (1 Samuel 8:19b–20)

God was displeased, but he told the prophet Samuel to accede to their demands:

And the LORD said to Samuel, "Obey the voice of the people in all that they say to you, for they have not rejected you, but they have rejected me from being king over them. According to all the deeds that they have done, from the day I brought them up out of Egypt even to this day, forsaking me and serving other gods, so they are also doing to you. Now then, obey their voice; only you shall solemnly warn them and show them the ways of the king who shall reign over them." (1 Samuel 8:7–9)

God knew that Israel had to learn a lesson. It was a lesson from which they would never recover. They would be ruled by kings until they were taken into captivity and then be an occupied nation, ruled by world powers, until Jerusalem was destroyed in AD70.

Did God care whether other nations had kings? Apparently not. There is no condemnation of any of the area nations for having a king. But for Israel, it was a lesson that God knew they needed to learn.

As the young mouse in the fable that began this chapter learned (all too late), there are innumerable lessons that only specific groups need to learn. Certain groups of people, based on race, nationality, religion, location, etc. may need to learn lessons that people in other groups of race, nationality religion, location, etc. may NOT need to learn.

Last there are **lessons that specific individuals need to learn.**

There are lessons that I need to learn that are unique to me. Oh, they may be similar to what others need to learn. But those others are not in the same situation I am in. They are not in the same relationships I am in. They do not have the same background and experiences that I do. So, while my lessons may be similar to the lessons that others need to learn, they are not exactly like those of anyone else.

For example, most husbands need to learn to communicate effectively with their wives. That would be a lesson that a group of people need to learn. But no one else on the planet is married to the woman I have been married to for the past 36 years. Because of her unique background, make-up, personality, etc. there are ways that I need to learn to react, to communicate, to listen, and to speak that may be different from what any other husband on earth may need to learn. (That is not a commentary on my wife except to say that she and all other wives are wonderfully unique.)

Again, there are spiritual lessons that I need to learn that you may or may not need to learn. Each of us are unique and if we believe that God loves each one of us individually, then he has specific lessons that he wants each one of us to learn.

- *"Before I formed you in the womb I knew you, and before you were born I consecrated you; I appointed you a prophet to the nations."* (Jeremiah 1:5)

- *For I know the plans I have for you, declares the LORD, plans for welfare and not for evil, to give you a future and a hope.* (Jeremiah 29:11)

I love the story at the end of the Gospel of John. It follows that tender story of the restoration of Peter. Peter had denied knowing Jesus on the night before Jesus' crucifixion. In an appearance after his resurrection, Jesus asks Peter to affirm his love for him three times…one time for every time he denied knowing Jesus. At the end of that beautiful interaction, Jesus warns Peter of the kind of death he will endure and then ends with the same words he used when he originally called Peter from a life of fishing: "Follow me."

Peter had just heard a prediction from Jesus of Peter's own old age and death. Peter looks over to John, the disciple whom Jesus loved. "When Peter saw him, he said to Jesus, "Lord, what about this man?" Jesus said to him, 'If it is my will that he remain until I come, what is that to you? You follow me!'" (John 21:21-22)

In other words, "Peter, I have lessons for you to learn. I have different lessons for John to learn. Your only responsibility is to follow me and to be obedient to the lessons that I have for you."

I may see lessons that a brother or sister need to learn. That is not my primary concern. My concern is to follow Christ and be obedient to the lessons that He has for me.

What They Need to Learn

So, while the horizontal axis of the "What Is God Teaching Us About" matrix deals with who is learning the lesson, the vertical axis of the matrix deals with what they need to learn. And as I said when I began this chapter, that list of lessons is innumerably long.

But I believe that they can be categorized into four categories.

LESSONS ABOUT
OURSELVES

LESSONS ABOUT
OTHERS

LESSONS ABOUT
LIFE

LESSONS ABOUT
GOD

Lessons about ourselves

Plato's words "Know thyself" have rung throughout the millennia since spoken, but are much easier to say than to do. One might think that this is a task for teenagers or young adults. Nothing could be farther from the truth. My life is a constant reminder to me of the truth of Henry and Richard Blackaby's words in *The Experience* when they say: "As you grow older, you'll realize more and more that you don't really know yourself the way you thought you did."[23]

Examples of lessons that we should learn about ourselves are:

- What we do well/what we don't do well.

- What we love in life.

- What motivates us

- How to function as an independently living human being.

- What angers us (and why).

- What things we are willing to tolerate in life and what

things we are not.

- What we value above other things.

- What we want to accomplish in life and why.

- Who we want to spend our time (even our life) with and why.

The list could go on and on. Each of us can ask ourselves: what lessons about myself have I learned recently? What lessons am I learning currently?

These questions point to the fact that there are lessons about ourselves that groups of people need to learn and lessons about ourselves that we, as individuals, need to learn.

A lesson that ancient Israel never seemed to get about itself was that God had created them as a people for several purposes, one of those was to be a blessing to the nations of the world. That is clearly evident both in the call of Abraham, but also in the Lord's words before the destruction of Sodom and Gomorrah:

Genesis 12:2–3: *"I will make you into a great nation, and I will bless you; I will make your name great, and you will be a blessing. I will bless those who bless you, and whoever curses you I will curse; and all peoples on earth will be blessed through you."*

Genesis 18:18: *Abraham will surely become a great and powerful nation, and all nations on earth will be blessed through him.*

Paul reaffirms that truth in Galatians 3:14: *"He redeemed us in order that the blessing given to Abraham might come to the Gentiles through Christ Jesus, so that by faith we might receive the promise of the Spirit."*

While all people are intended to be a blessing to others in certain ways, Israel needed to learn that one of their purposes of their selection as God's chosen people was so that they would be a blessing to all of the nations of the world.

Lessons about others

God recognized that humans isolated as individuals was not good. And so he created Eve to accompany Adam. Since that time there have been important lessons for us to learn about others.

Examples of lessons that we should learn about others might include:

- The ability to see others as valuable in their own right and not only as they serve our needs.

- The ability to treat others with kindness and respect.

- The importance of community.

- The realization that not everyone sees things the same way, and that fact is often neither right nor wrong.

- The skill of being able to "read" other people's emotions and non-verbal cues.

- How heart to have empathy for others.

- The awareness that "others" includes spiritual beings (including Satan)

We also learn about other people as persons. John D. Mayer in his blog "The Personality Analyst" on the Psychology Today website names stages in getting to know a person. There is the stage of:

1. Learning from Afar. (We learn about or are told by others things about someone we have yet to meet)

2. First Impressions. (What we observe when we first meet that person and our reaction to what we observe)

3. Ongoing Observation. (No one can hold up a façade forever. As we interact with a person, we learn many new things about them…some good, some not as good)

4. Testing and Checking. (We learn about others by testing what we have observed to see if it holds true in differing

situations).

5. Last Memories. We hold on to recollections and impressions of people when they are gone from us…either temporarily or permanently.[24]

There are things about others that a specific group needs to know while those outside that group do not. In my family I, my wife, my two sons, my two daughters-in-law and my grandchildren need to know one another in ways that no one else in the world really needs to know.

Likewise there are lessons I, as an individual, need to learn about others that other people may or may not need to learn about those around them.

Lessons about life

While I don't agree with everything on his list, Phil McGraw [aka Dr. Phil] in his book, *Life Strategies* lists lessons that we should learn about life. (See chart on next page)

In each case, there are life lessons all people need to learn, life lessons certain groups of people need to learn, and life lessons that individuals need to learn.

A life lesson that I needed to learn came in the form of a book recommended to me shortly after I was let go at the church. A friend who had been in similar circumstances, recommended the book, *When God Has Put You on Hold* by Bill Austin. His entire thesis is based on Jeremiah's letter to the elders in Jer. 29:1-14. In his excellent book, Austin talks about the importance of accepting the reality of things. That doesn't just include accepting that we are in the situation that we are in, but also accepting the reality that God wants to use ALL the times in our lives, not just the times of active engagement. He states,

"The tragedy of most mean-times is that we do not see them as real life: they are just gaps or voids to be endured until we can get back to our real life. But in reality, this meantime may furnish us our greatest opportunity for service or influence."[25]

I needed to hear that during the "what now?" section of our life after leaving pastoral ministry. It was a life lesson that I know I needed to learn, and I suspect there were others that needed to learn it as well (the mere existence of Austin's book is indicative of that).

Lessons about God

Continuing to fill out our matrix, there are lessons that individuals, groups of people and all people need to learn about themselves, others, and life as well as lessons to be learned about God.

Dr. Phil's Ten Life Laws

Life Law #1: You either get it or you don't.
> Strategy: Become one of those who gets it.

Life Law #2: You create your own experience.
> Strategy: Acknowledge and accept accountability for your life. Understand your role in creating results.

Life Law #3: People do what works.
> Strategy: Identify the payoffs that drive your behavior and that of others.

Life Law #4: You cannot change what you do not acknowledge.
> Strategy: Get real with yourself about life and everybody in it. Be truthful about what isn't working in your life. Stop making excuses and start making results.

Life Law #5: Life rewards action.
> Strategy: Make careful decisions and then pull the trigger. Learn that the world couldn't care less about thoughts without actions.

Life Law #6: You know and experience this world only through the perceptions that you create.
> Strategy: Identify the filters through which you view the world. Acknowledge your history without being controlled by it.

Life Law #7: Life is managed; it is not cured.
> Strategy: Learn to take charge of your life and hold on. This is a long ride, and you are the driver every single day.

Life Law #8: We teach people how to treat us.
> Strategy: Own, rather than complain about, how people treat

---

Dr. Phil's Ten Life Laws (cont.)

you. Learn to renegotiate your relationships to have what you want.

Life Law #9: There is power in forgiveness.

Strategy: Open your eyes to what anger and resentment are doing to you. Take your power back from those who have hurt you.

Life Law #10: You have to name it before you can claim it.

Strategy: Get clear about what you want and take your turn. Life is not always fair.

There can be no doubt that God wants us to come to a knowledge of Himself. Earlier in this chapter, I quoted I Tim 2:3b-4 which says, *"God our Savior…wants all people to be saved and to come to a knowledge of the truth."*

Examples of lessons that we should all learn about God are:

- That God exists.

- How he manifests himself.

- God's character and glory.

- God's purposes.

- How to be in unity with God.

- What types of actions please/displease God and why?

- What God promises.

There were specific lessons that God wants certain people to learn. He wanted ancient Israel to learn certain lessons that were not so relevant to other societies. As we will see in a later chapter, He wants leaders to learn certain lessons that followers may not need to learn. He wants husbands to learn certain things about Himself with which wives may not need to be so familiar.

And there are specific lessons about Him that He wants you or me to learn that are unique to my situation, personality or history.

One of the most beautiful passages about coming to know God is found in the epilogue to Thomas Merton's autobiography, *The Seven Storey Mountain*. Merton was a Catholic priest and mystic. After telling of his journey both to faith as well as to the priesthood, Merton speaks of the tension between learning who we are and learning who God is.

> You have called me here not to wear a label by which I can recognize myself and place myself in some kind of a category. You do not want me to be thinking about what I am, but about what You are. Or rather, You do not even want me to be thinking about anything much: for You would raise me above the level of thought. And if I am always trying to figure out what I am and where I am and why I am, how will that work be done?

> I do not make a big drama of this business. I do not say: "You have asked me for everything, and I have renounced all." Because I no longer desire to see anything that implies a distance between You and me: and if I stand back and consider myself and You as if something had passed between us, from me to You, I will inevitably see the gap between us and remember the distance between us.

> My God, it is that gap and that distance which kill me.

> That is the only reason why I desire solitude—to be lost to all created things, to die to them and to the knowledge of them, for they remind me of my distance from You. They tell me something about You: that You are far from them, even though You are in them. You have made them and Your presence sustains their being, and they hide You from me. And I would

have alone, and out of them. *O beata solitudo!*[26]

	LESSONS ALL PEOPLE MUST LEARN	LESSONS SPECIFIC GROUPS OF PEOPLE MUST LEARN	LESSONS SPECIFIC INDIVIDUALS MUST LEARN
LESSONS ABOUT **OURSELVES**	LESSONS ALL PEOPLE MUST LEARN ABOUT THEMSELVES	LESSONS SPECIFIC GROUPS OF PEOPLE MUST LEARN ABOUT THEMSELVES	LESSONS SPECIFIC INDIVIDUALS MUST LEARN ABOUT THEMSELVES
LESSONS ABOUT **OTHERS**	LESSONS ALL PEOPLE MUST LEARN ABOUT OTHERS	LESSONS SPECIFIC GROUPS OF PEOPLE MUST LEARN ABOUT OTHERS	LESSONS SPECIFIC INDIVIDUALS MUST LEARN ABOUT OTHERS
LESSONS ABOUT **LIFE**	LESSONS ALL PEOPLE MUST LEARN ABOUT LIFE	LESSONS SPECIFIC GROUPS OF PEOPLE MUST LEARN ABOUT LIFE	LESSONS SPECIFIC INDIVIDUALS MUST LEARN ABOUT LIFE
LESSONS ABOUT **GOD**	LESSONS ALL PEOPLE MUST LEARN ABOUT GOD	LESSONS SPECIFIC GROUPS OF PEOPLE MUST LEARN ABOUT GOD	LESSONS SPECIFIC INDIVIDUALS MUST LEARN ABOUT GOD

Putting the two axes of the matrix together, we get:

3D Teachability

To add one more layer of complexity to the question, it is not just "who needs to learn the lesson?" and not just "what the lesson is about?" that needs to be learned, but in addition it matters "what is the source of the lesson?".

For example…

- There are lessons all specific people need to learn about themselves from God.

- There are lessons all specific people need to learn about themselves from others.

- There are lessons all specific people need to learn about themselves from themselves.

- There are lessons all specific people need to learn about themselves from life.

Furthermore,

- There are lessons all people need to learn about others from God

- There are lessons all people need to learn about others from others

- There are lessons all people need to learn about others from themselves.

- There are lessons all people need to learn about others from life.

In other words, let's take that graph that we have above and turn it sideways:

It could be depicted graphically like this:

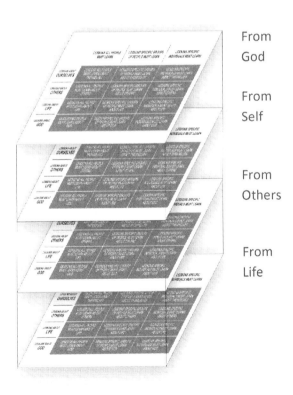

From God

From Self

From Others

From Life

Some would say that in reality all the lessons that we learn are from God, but this is not the case. That is one reason why I believe that this matrix is extremely helpful.

Let's look at the premise: "Some people need to learn that God does not exist." It is a legitimate statement, but when we add the third-dimensional aspect to it (from where is that lesson coming?) that the matter actually becomes clearer. Does that statement come from God, others, me or life? Obviously if God doesn't exist, the lesson doesn't come from Him! Does the lesson come from others, from me or from life? If it is coming from myself, upon what evidence am I basing that? Is my information about that (or the existence of any other) evidence complete? Does it arise from life? How does life teach that, and is that verifiable? Others may want me to learn that God does not exist. What might be the motives of others in promoting that statement?

An event that arose during my youth reminds me of the importance of "considering the source". During Junior High I had done something (I am still not exactly sure what) to earn the wrath of a group of bullies at our Junior High. Every day, they would wait after school and try to beat me up. I began to take various routes home from school (carrying my French Horn case!) in order to avoid being beaten up. While I lived a block away from school, I would often walk MILES in order to get home through various circuitous routes. This went on for several months until my mother, knowing what was happening, but being unable to do anything else about it, took me to the principal of the school and asked if I should take self-defense lessons. He was horrified. "Absolutely not!" was his reply. "Just ignore them and they will go away!" (Of course that was what I had been trying to do for months). It was horrible advice. What I should have done was learned skills, both verbal and physical, to stop the attacks. But since the principal was an authority figure, we accepted what he said. What he said was wrong. Using this template, it is important to "consider the source". What motives did he have for rejecting the idea that I should learn self-defense skills? To maintain peace at his school and keep fights from happening? Of course fights were already happening.

If I had objectively "considered the source" or looked at from where the lesson was coming, I could have better evaluated (and ultimately rejected) it.

Conclusion

This has been a complex chapter (at least to write, and I suspect to read!) Part of that comes from the very first observations with which I opened this chapter: "This is the chapter that can't really be written…. To make a list of lessons everyone needs to learn would be impossible."

But that doesn't excuse us from thinking through the subject and seeing if there are categories of lessons. And there are.

I am always chastened by the story Charles Colson tells:

Chuck Colson writes of being invited to preach at tough old San Quentin Prison, an opportunity he greatly anticipated and carefully planned for. Three hundred of the 2,200 inmates had agreed to come to the chapel to hear him. But just days before his arrival, officials uncovered a hidden cache of weapons, and the prison was immediately locked down with inmates confined to their cells.

When Colson arrived at the prison chapel, he was disheartened to find that only a handful of men were able to be present, and they were mostly Christians. His spirits flagged, for he had so hoped to preach the gospel to the unsaved. Struggling with a lack of enthusiasm, he thought Maybe I'll just give a short devotional, ten minutes or so. I can't really preach my heart out to this crowd.

But spotting a video camera in the far end of the room, he said to himself, Maybe this is being recorded for the chapel library. Maybe

I'd better give it my all. He felt convicted for basing his morale and mood on the outer circumstances rather than the inner impulse of the Spirit, and so he preached with great fervor, as though a thousand inmates were listening.

Later he mentioned to the prison chaplain how disappointed he had been to have missed sharing the gospel with the three hundred men who had originally signed up to attend. "Didn't you know?" asked the chaplain. "Because of the lockdown, the administration agreed to videotape your sermon. They'll be showing it to all the inmates tomorrow on closed-circuit television in the morning and again in the afternoon."

In fact, the sermon was aired not just twice, but nearly a dozen times over the following weeks. Because of the lockdown, not just three hundred but all 2,200 prisoners heard the gospel.

Colson said that he learned three lessons from the incident:

- WHO NEEDED TO LEARN THE LESSON?: Charles Colson

- WHAT WAS THE LESSON ABOUT?:

    o God calls us to faithfulness, not to success.

    o When our goal is to change society, we often fail. When it is simple obedience to God, He blesses our efforts more than we can envision.

    o We should not grow weary in well-doing, for we shall reap a harvest if we faint not.

- WHO/WHAT WAS THE SOURCE OF THE LESSON?: Mother Teresa. [27]

Chapter 3: Questions for Personal Thought and Group Discussion

- Give some examples of universal lessons that you have learned.

- To what groups do you belong (family in all its different dimensions? employer? employee? citizen? church member? this list goes on and on.)
  - What lessons are unique to that group of people?
  - Which ones have you learned?
  - Which ones are you still working to learn?

- List ten things about yourself that are different from other people:
  - What lessons have you had to learn individually because of that? Which lessons are you still working to learn?
  - What lessons have been the most difficult for you to learn?

- Have you stopped learning about yourself? Why or why not? If you have, what can you do to change that?

- What was your reaction to Dr.Phil's Ten Life Laws? Which one or two do you struggle with the most? What can you do today to better learn that lesson(s)?

- How have you learned most of your lessons about God?

- Are there lessons about God that you have had to relearn because you learned a wrong lesson?

- Why is the third dimension of asking from whom the lesson comes important?

Fable #4: The Salmon Who Almost Had Too Much Success

A young salmon was coming to the mouth of the river that poured out into the wide ocean beyond. As she grew in her excitement, she did not want to listen to the advice of one of the older salmon who was returning from the sea.

"You are not yet prepared to go out into the ocean. It is very dangerous for you to go out there." warned the mature salmon.

"But I have faced danger before and always been successful. When I was newly hatched and only a fry, I was successfully able to hide under the gravel until I had eaten all the nourishment in my yolk sac. No one could find me there, and I had all I wanted. But now, I want to be out in the ocean!"

"Oh, but you are not under the gravel feasting on your yolk sac anymore," came the reply of the wise experienced salmon.

"But that is not all," cried the impatient smolt. "When my yolk sac was empty I came up and was able to find lots of plants and insects and larvae to enjoy. I grew these beautiful parr stripes on my sides which disguise me from ducks and herons so they cannot eat me. I will be fine in the ocean!"

"Oh, my dear parr salmon, you do not understand. You must drink lots and lots of water out in the ocean."

"But I've always had enough water. I LIVE in water! I've never had to drink water before—I get all the water I need from what I eat. I will get enough water in the ocean."

"Oh, foolish parr salmon. You do not understand. The river has no salt. But the ocean is filled with salt. The salt from the water will accumulate in your body. You must allow time for your body to learn to hold on to the water and expel the salt. Otherwise you will dry out and die. You must wait here at the mouth of the river and let your body become accustomed to slightly higher levels of salt before you can go out into the ocean with its much higher levels of salt."

"But I want to be free! I want to be in the wideness and depth of the ocean! I don't want to wait. I have been successful as a fry, I have been successful as a smolt, I have been successful as a parr. I will be successful in the ocean."

Day after day the parr salmon argued with the older salmon about allowing her to leave the mouth of the river and venture out into the ocean. Finally, the cautious older fish consented and the young salmon ventured out into the wideness of the ocean.

Soon she was glad that the older fish had delayed her. Other impatient parr salmon who did not have such a wise advisor had rushed out from the river before they knew how to adjust to the salt water of the ocean. Most became very sick and many died. Their many successes in the past were not enough to save them in this new environment.

Moral: Past success can sometimes be a deterrent to future success.

Chapter 4: HINDRANCES TO TEACHABILITY: Why might I lack a teachable Spirit?

"Only one thing in history is certain: that mankind is unteachable,"
--Winston Churchill, 1941
"There are some people that if they don't know, you can't tell them."
--Louis Armstrong

For up to six centuries the stone tablet had stood on the hillside. No one could point with certainty to when it had been erected, but it had been there as long as anyone could remember. And even though they did not know who erected it, the people of the little village of Aneyoshi obeyed its instructions: "Do not build your homes below this point!"

There were hundreds of these so-called "tsunami stones" along the coast of Japan. They stood as silent sentries, a message from generations gone that when a tsunami came, it could come as far as that marker. The last major tsunami had happened in 1896 and had killed 22,000 people.

Modern builders were confident that their new building techniques and seawalls had made the tsunami stones irrelevant. And so they ignored the stones, some of which stood up to 10 feet tall.

When the giant Tōhoku tsunami came on March 11, 2011, devastation reigned. When totals finally came in, the tsunami had left 15,882 people dead, 6,142 injured, and 2,668 to be declared missing across twenty prefectures. 129,225 buildings totally collapsed, with a further 254,204 buildings 'half collapsed', and another 691,766 buildings partially damaged.

In the village of Aneyoshi, however, the 11 households were

safe and dry. The waves stopped just 300 feet below the stone, and the village beyond it.

The story of Tōhoku hauntingly reminded me of Pearl S. Buck's book *The Big Wave*. Pearl Buck was the daughter of missionaries to China, and bases the story on her own experience watching a tsunami destroy a fishing village. The Big Wave tells the story of two Japanese boys, Kino and Jiya. Kino's family farms and lives high on the hill, but Jiya's family fishes and lives in the fishing village built on the beach. All of the people, those who live on the beach and those who live higher know of the danger of a "big wave" (tsunami). Jiya says, "Sometimes the old ocean god begins to roll in his ocean bed and to heave up his head and shoulders, and the waves run back and forth. Then he stands upright and roars and the earth shakes under the water."

And, of course in the book, a tsunami comes. The entire village on the beach with all of the fishermen and their families are swept away to their deaths. Jiya, who has fled to Kino's house is adopted by Kino's family as their own son because all of his family has been killed.

Toward the end of the book an ominous event happens:

Kino saw that Jiya always looked out of the door every morning and he looked at the empty beach, searching with his eyes as though something might one day come back. One day he did see something. Kino was at the door putting on his shoes and he heard Jiya cry out in a loud voice, "Kino, come here!" Quickly Kino went and Jiya pointed down the hillside. "Look is someone building a house on the beach?"

Kino looked and saw that indeed it was so. Two men were pounding posts into the sand, and a woman and a child stood near, watching. "Can it be that they will build again on the beach.'" he exclaimed.

But they could not rest with watching. They ran down the hill to the beach and went to the two men. "Are you building a house?" Jiya cried.

The men paused and the elder one nodded. "Our father used to live here and we with him. During these years we have lived in the outhouses of the castle and we have fished from other shores. Now we are tired of having no homes of our own. Besides, this is still the best of all beaches for fishing."

"But what if the big wave comes back?" Kino asked.

The men shrugged their shoulders. "There was a big wave in our great-grandfather's time. All the houses were swept away, but our grandfather came back. In our father's time the big wave came again, but now we come back."

"What of your children?" Kino asked anxiously.

"The big wave may never come back," the men said. And they began to pound the post into the sand again.

All this time Jiya had not said another word. He stood watching the work, his face musing and strange. The big wave and the sorrow it had brought had changed him forever. Never again would he laugh easily or talk carelessly. He had learned to live with his parents and his brother dead, as Kino's father had said he would, and he did not weep. He thought of them every day and he did not feel they were far from him or he from them. Their faces, their voices, the way his father talked and looked, his mother's smile, his brother's laughter, all were with him still and would be forever."[28]

At the end of the book, in spite of the devastation that he had seen from the tsunami that had occurred, Jiya (who has by this time married Kino's little sister) joined the other villagers in building a house on the beach, knowing the danger, but confident that it couldn't happen again "to them."

What is it that makes us ignore the warnings of life? Why are we often so unteachable? Or, in my case, why am I often so unteachable?

The subject of why we may be unteachable is not a positive topic. As I was writing this book and describing it to another coach, she said, "Focus only on the positive." But the reality is that unless we know what the barriers are, we may hit our heads again and again without being willing/able to remove the barriers.

The reality is that we may not be able to rid ourselves of all of the hindrances completely, but as we address them we become more open to being teachable. Do not become discouraged if you are still struggling with an area of hindrance in your life. Time, prayer and effort can help the barriers eventually come down.

There are usually multiple barriers to teachableness and often they are a mixture of reasons, but I believe that eight reasons are worth raising up:

Pride

Probably the main reason, and the core of many of the other reasons I will list is pride. The people of Israel are the classic story of people who were unteachable because of pride.

In 2 Kings 17, the writer describes the demise of the northern kingdom of Israel. Israel had not really been a free nation even at that point. Assyria dominated the nation to the point that Israel paid annual tribute money.

But when Shalmaneser, king of Assyria discovered that Hoshea, king of Israel had stopped paying tribute money and instead was seeking an alliance with Egypt, he attacked. He imprisoned Hoshea and lay siege to the country for three years. 2 Kings 17:6 records that the inhabitants of Samaria were deported to the town of Gozan in the region of Hazan, northeast of Nineveh.

The writer then (vv. 7-23) summarizes God's case against the Israelites: his justification for allowing the nation to be conquered and the citizens deported. In vv. 7-12 he lists the sins and transgressions of the nation. In v. 13 he records the warnings of the Lord: *"The LORD warned Israel and Judah through all his prophets and seers: 'Turn from your evil ways. Observe my commands and decrees, in accordance with the entire Law that I commanded your ancestors to obey and that I delivered to you through my servants the prophets.'"*

He then concludes with the sad evaluation: *"But they would not listen and were as stiff-necked as their ancestors, who did not trust in the LORD their God."* (v. 14).

It was not simply for their sins that God's judgment came upon them. It was for their stubborn refusal to be teachable: their unwillingness to obey and trust God.

After the return of Israel from exile, the priest Ezra called for a national day of repentance. On that day he said, in part, *"But they, our ancestors, became arrogant and stiff-necked, and did not obey your commands.... You warned them in order to turn them back to your law, but they became arrogant and disobeyed your commands. They sinned against your ordinances, of which you said, 'Whoever obeys them will live by them.' Stubbornly they turned their backs on you, became stiff-necked and refused to listen."* (Nehemiah 9:16, 29)

The *Dictionary of Biblical Imagery* describe the term "stiff-necked" this way:

The outward posture of the neck is often used in the Bible to indicate the inward orientation of one's heart. The metaphor of being "stiff-necked" is used frequently to describe Israel's resistance to God's lordship over the nation (Ex 32:9; 33:5; Neh 9:29; Jer 7:26; Acts 7:51). Isaiah employs the image *of "walking along with outstretched necks"* to portray the self-centered arrogance and defiant unconcern for injustice of the women of Jerusalem (Is 3:16; cf. Ps 75:5).[29]

In brief, a "stiff neck" is an image of refusing to change one's behavior or direction of life. They will not bend in submission or turn to the right or to the left. They are determined to go one way—their own way.

Sometimes pride manifests itself as an unwillingness to learn from a certain type of person, or a person from people of a certain age, gender, educational level, culture, tribe or social status.

The Pastor of Hope Chapel in Dallas TX, Harold Bullock tells the story of the plastic fork. If you were truly hungry and you were presented with a wonderful meal and a plastic fork, would you refuse to eat the meal until you had been given a silver metal fork? Likely not. If you did, you probably were not all that hungry. But the hungrier you are, the less the utensil matters.

Bullock notes that there are lots of Christians who would be delighted to be personally taught by Dr. Billy Graham. But are you just as eager to learn from the leader of your home Bible study? What about your parents? Your spouse? Your kids? Your roommates? Your enemies?

"If you won't eat with the plastic, God won't set out the silver",[30] declares Bullock.

There is a lot of elitism in today's church. Too many Christians are proud that they listen to specific speakers regularly on TV or the internet or radio. They attend the mega church, or the missional church or the "gospel-centered" church. They are always quoting the pastor of the huge church or the writer of latest bestselling book.

But they are not as eager to listen to someone else who has fewer degrees, less prestige, less renown. Bullock notes, "If you're really teachable, the person who is teaching you doesn't have to be famous…just right."

Fear

A second hindrance to teachableness is fear. Fear? You might think that fear would be a reason to BE teachable...you are afraid of being wrong...of making a mistake...you want to know what is true and right and so you become teachable.

But more often than not, fear leads to unteachableness.

The Roman governor Pilate is an example of this. After Jesus' arrest Pilate questioned Jesus and declared to the Jewish leaders that he found no reason to find Jesus guilty of a capital offense. The Jewish leaders continued to push him, to the point that *"when Pilate heard this, he was more afraid than ever."* (John 19:8) Refusing to consider the claims of Jesus because of his fear of the Jews, Pilate turned Jesus over for crucifixion.

Of what are we afraid?

I think my reaction to my early history made it harder for me to be teachable. When I was very young, whatever assertions others who were in authority in my life said, was true. The current stereotypes of the 1950s and early 60s are certainly exaggerations, but people were taught to follow the norms.

I was born the son of the principal at our local public school who was also the preacher at our church. My dad served part-time at a little country church that we attended while his full-time job was as principal of the town's only public school.

I was fairly smart. (At least all the evidence at the time pointed that way). I got very good grades in school. I was always seemingly one of the favorites of my teachers (the fact that their favor may have been tied to the fact that my dad was their boss never occurred to me until I was an adult...seriously!) For a long time I was extremely proud that I had been one of the champion spellers at our small town school and went to the county spelling bee! (The fact that I didn't place in the top 10 finishers at the county level was obviously a fault of the system or maybe I had just had an off day).

I wasn't necessarily cocky. I just knew the way things were. My dad was the authority and I accepted that. Everybody in town seemed to know my dad and I (by extension) was important because I was his son.

But then, something happened. We moved from the small town where I had been born to a much larger town north of Denver, CO. Before, I had been a big fish in a small pond, now I was a (very) small fish in a big pond. I was angry when I started getting B+s instead of As on my report cards. But culturally everything seemed different. From a community of descendants of northern European immigrants, where we moved was much more multi-ethnic. I attended a school where no one knew my dad. The church we attended was 10 times the size of our rural church in Kansas, and my dad wasn't the preacher.

And then ten months after we moved to Colorado, my dad died. He was 31 when he died and I had just turned 11. Everything in my world turned upside down. Instead of the comfort of a small Kansas farming community where everyone knew my dad, now we lived in a (comparatively) larger city where not only did people not know my dad, but I had no dad. We went from comfortable middle-class to very poor.

And this was during the 1960s…one of the most traumatic decades in our nation's history. Culturally, the upheaval of the 1960s is often said to have begun with the assassination of President Kennedy in 1963 and concluded with the resignation of President Nixon in 1974. (We moved to Colorado in 1966, dad died in 1967 and I graduated from high school in 1974—right in that tumultuous window.) We lived in fifteen miles northeast of Boulder, CO which was, in the 1960s, one of the epicenters of the drug and hippie counter-culture.

America in the 1960s was a confusing place in which to live: The assassination of President Kennedy and his brother Robert Kennedy; the Civil Rights movement, including riots and marches, and the assassination of Martin Luther King; the fear of the spread of communism acerbated by the Cuban Missile crisis, the invasion of Czechoslovakia by the Russians and a "space race" against the Soviets to the moon; the growing involvement of the US in the war in Vietnam and increasing public disenchantment with and opposition to the war; the rise of rampant and more public use of illicit drugs; the changing attitudes toward sexuality, sparked at least in part, by the approval in 1960 of public use of female birth control pills; the rise of atheism in America, with the Supreme court decisions in 1962, 1963 and 1971 outlawing Christian prayer and the religious study of the Bible in public schools; the rise of the "God is Dead" theology popularized by the cover article of *Time* magazine edition of April 8, 1966 emblazoned with the question, "Is God Dead?" All of these were a part of my consciousness.

Our family and our church, while not exactly fundamentalist, certainly were on the conservative end of the evangelical Christian spectrum. The national church body of which our church had been a part had a hugely traumatic split in the mid-60s that basically split the denomination in half: conservative versus liberal.

That, and more, caused many (including me) to "hunker down". My unspoken attitude (and the unspoken attitude of many others) was "You cannot afford to be teachable because you cannot admit being wrong. If you are wrong in one area, all the dominoes in your belief system will topple and confusion and chaos will result."

It was a time when it was too easy to be suspicious of change and anything new: not fertile ground for teachableness. There were certainly specific instances of teachableness, but to hold on to what we knew seemed to be more important. It was easy to simply cling to the things that we knew were true and unchanging. With the death of my dad, to defend what I believed he had thought made me less open to other ways of thinking. It was a loyalty factor. There became a real dichotomy of "the evil that is out there" with the "good that is in here". To know what you were "against" was at least as important as knowing what you were "for". When you are insecure, like I often am, you hold on to your positions because they define you.

My value was threatened.

- If my value came from being my dad's son…that was gone.

- If my value came from being in a small town where everyone knew who you were…that was gone.

- If my value came from being a top student in my school…that was gone.

- If my value came from economic security…that was gone.

- If my value came from holding a certain set of religious or philosophical beliefs…those were being challenged more and more every day.

We may be afraid of many things, but underlying them all is a desire to look good before others instead of before God. We tend to be man-pleasers (look good) rather than learn. Perhaps Paul was accused of this when he responded to the Galatians: *"Am I now trying to win the approval of human beings, or of God? Or am I trying to please people? If I were still trying to please people, I would not be a servant of Christ."* (Gal 1.10).

The old fashioned term for this is being a "man-pleaser". (The term is derived from the King James translation of Gal. 1.10). We may be afraid of being shown to be uninformed. We want to APPEAR informed rather than admit our ignorance. Again, that gets back to looking look good before others instead of before God. We may need to justify ourselves and previous actions. Self-justification is the enemy of teachableness.

Laziness

It may sound blunt, but sometimes we are unteachable because we are lazy. Either we are too lazy to learn, or we recognize that if we learn, it will necessitate us changing our behavior, and changing our behavior is just too much work.

In Proverbs 12:15, the writer tells us *"The way of fools seems right to them, but the wise listen to advice."*

Again Solomon says: *"Lazy people consider themselves smarter than seven wise counselors."* (Prov. 26:16, NLT)

Just two chapters earlier, Solomon had described the lazy person:

I went past the field of a sluggard, past the vineyard of someone who has no sense; thorns had come up everywhere, the ground was covered with weeds, and the stone wall was in ruins. I applied my heart to what I observed and learned a lesson from what I saw: A little sleep, a little slumber, a little folding of the hands to rest—and poverty will come on you like a thief and scarcity like an armed man. (Prov. 24:30-34)

Laziness will keep us from being teachable—it is just too much work!

I see this as one of the dangers of our current era. While we may not call it "sloth", we are allowing the mind-numbing sameness of "entertainment" to keep us from learning much besides what the entertainment world wants us to know.

What Neil Postman said of western society in 1985 could just as accurately be said of the church today: In his important book, *Amusing Ourselves to Death*, Postman notes that while many feared that western culture would be destroyed by an Orwellian dictatorship *ala 1984*, the real problem was predicted by Aldous Huxley in *Brave New World*. Postman comments:

What Huxley teaches is that in the age of advanced technology, spiritual devastation is more likely to come from an enemy with a smiling face than from one whose countenance exudes suspicion and hate. In the Huxleyan prophecy, Big Brother does not watch us, by his choice. We watch him, by ours. There is no need for wardens or gates or Ministries of Truth. When a population becomes distracted by trivia, when cultural life is redefined as a perpetual round of entertainments, when serious public conversation becomes a form of baby-talk, when, in short, a people become an audience and their public business a vaudeville act, then a nation finds itself at risk; culture-death is a clear possibility.[31]

We may not like to think of the barrage of amusements and entertainments that fill our lives as a form of laziness, but their effect is exactly the same.

Complaining and Criticizing

The chronic complainer or critic is also often unteachable. Some people are always looking for things that are wrong. They are not looking to change. They are not looking to adjust or learn new ways of doing things. The complainer simply wants to protest that things are not the way he or she think it should be.

The story of the Israelites in the desert is full of examples of complaining:

Now the people complained about their hardships in the hearing of the LORD, and when He heard them his anger was aroused. Then fire from the LORD burned among them and consumed some of the outskirts of the camp. When the people cried out to Moses, he prayed to the LORD and the fire died down. So that place was called Taberah, because fire from the LORD had burned among them. The rabble with them began to crave other food, and again the Israelites started wailing and said, "If only we had meat to eat! We remember the fish we ate in Egypt at no cost—also the cucumbers, melons, leeks, onions and garlic. But now we have lost our appetite; we never see anything but this manna!" The manna was like coriander seed and looked like resin. The people went around gathering it, and then ground it in a hand mill or crushed it in a mortar. They cooked it in a pot or made it into loaves. And it tasted like something made with olive oil. When the dew settled on the camp at night, the manna also came down. Moses heard the people of every family wailing at the entrance to their tents. The LORD became exceedingly angry, and Moses was troubled. (Numbers 11:1-10)

There was no desire to be teachable and learn lessons either from God, or their circumstances. The complainers revealed the unteachableness of their hearts.

Sin's Deceitfulness

But encourage one another daily, as long as it is called "Today," so that none of you may be hardened by sin's deceitfulness. (Heb. 3:13)

Another cause of unteachableness is the deceitfulness of sin. Sin clouds our judgment and warps our thinking. Sin takes our eyes off of God and puts it on ourselves. Even when the lesson is about me, my thinking needs to be just as much (or more) on God than it is on me.

That is the nature of ALL sin: taking our eyes off of God and putting it on something else. We cannot see God or our circumstances except through the filter of whatever it is that is primarily before our eyes.

How does sin deceive us? I can think of at least six ways:

1. **Sin lies to us about the character of God.** Satan has been using this lie as far back as the Garden of Eden. He sought to get Eve to question God's character. It seeks to make us believe that God does not love us. Sin seeks to make the holiness of God unattractive. Sin tries to get us to believe that God and his demands are unreasonable.

2. **Sin minimizes the significance of sin.** It leads us to believe that there is no reason for us to feel guilty--others

have done just as bad or worse. John Owen in *Indwelling Sin in Believers* notes that sin causes us to push the boundaries of grace beyond what God allows.

3. **It takes our eyes off of God and his promises.** We, rather than God, become the center of our attention. Sin is basically idolatry—our focus is on anything else rather than on God.

4. **Sin causes us to focus on the present instead of the eventual results/outcome of the sin.** It gives us short-term memories. Sin denies or minimizes any penalty for sin.

5. **Sin always presents unreal promises.** It promises satisfaction that it can never bring.

6. **Sin tells us lies about ourselves.** It makes us whitewash our motives. It makes us think that as long as we haven't sinned outwardly, that everything is OK.

Callousness--A Hard Heart

Proverbs 28:14: *Blessed is the one who always trembles before God, but whoever hardens their heart falls into trouble.*

The panoply of villains and antiheroes in literature and in the movies is huge. From Dr. Hannibal Lecter (*Silence of the Lambs*) to Sweeney Todd (*Sweeney Todd, the Demon Barber of Fleet Street*) to Darth Vader (*Star Wars*) to Mr. Potter (*It's a Wonderful Life*) to Valdemort (*Harry Potter*) to Iago (*Othello*) our desire to see the world in black and white terms remains undimmed.

A common theme running through these (and most) villains is their callous, hardheartedness.

In his classic *Paradise Lost*, John Milton depicts Satan as standing over a vast army of fallen angels, demons and false gods from around the known world. As he looks over the army at his command,

> "He through the armed files
> Darts his experienced eye, and soon traverse
> The whole Battalion views, their order due,
> Their visages and stature as of Gods,
> Their number last he sums. And now his heart
> Distends with pride, and hardening in his strength Glories...."
>
> (Lines 567-573)

"His heart distends with pride, and hardening in his strength Glories...." No more fitting description can be said of many of us who struggle with hardheartedness and callousness.

Hardness of heart and callousness would seem to be the opposite of teachableness.

One definition of "hard-hearted" is found in the *Dictionary of Bible Themes:* "Primarily, in Scripture, a persistent inner refusal to hear and obey the word of God. Also, in a more general sense, an uncaring or unsympathetic attitude towards other people".[32]

The "heart" is the word picture that the Bible uses to describe "the total inner self, a person's hidden core of being."[33] It involves the intellectual self, the emotional self, the volitional self, and the moral self. The spiritual writer Henri Nouwen says, "By 'heart' I mean the centre of our being, the place where we are most ourselves, where we are the most human, where we are most real."[34]

A hard heart is that part of our life becoming desensitized. That "inner self, the hidden core of being" can be hardened by intellectual, emotional or volitional decisions. One big way the heart is hardened is through disobedience or continued sin.

The classic example of the hardened heart is that of Pharaoh at the time of the Exodus, but many people are described as having hard hearts: Israel, the Pharisees, Jesus' disciples, and others.

How does a hard heart come? Often from a refusal to obey.

The example of Pharaoh is instructive. It seems like there is a conflict over the cause of Pharaoh's hard heart. Sometimes it says that God hardened Pharaoh's heart; other times it says that Pharaoh himself hardened his heart. Which is it?

I personally believe it is fairly plain in the text.

If you know the story, Moses was sent back to Egypt to demand that the Jewish people (the Hebrews) be set free from their slavery. God warned Moses that he would be unsuccessful in getting Pharaoh to change his mind, because *"The LORD said to Moses, 'When you return to Egypt, see that you perform before Pharaoh all the wonders I have given you the power to do. But I will harden his heart so that he will not let the people go.'"* (Exodus 4:21; see also 7:3). God was giving Moses an overview of the end result of the process.

Moses went to Pharaoh and demanded that Pharaoh set God's people free. Pharaoh, predictably, refused. God had told Moses that when Pharaoh initially refused he was to throw down his staff and it would turn into a serpent. Moses did so, but Pharaoh's magicians were able to duplicate the "trick". And so, we read, *"Pharaoh hardened his heart and would not listen even though God through Moses turned staff to snake and back."* (Exodus 7:13)

Strike one.

And so, God brought upon Pharaoh and Egypt ten increasingly terrible plagues to demonstrate God's power.

1.   There was the plague of turning all the water in Egypt to blood. After Pharaoh's magicians duplicated the act (don't ask me where they got the water, since apparently all the water had been turned to blood), so Pharaoh would not change his mind: *"But the Egyptian magicians did the same things by their secret arts, and Pharaoh's heart became hard; he would not listen to Moses and Aaron, just as the LORD had said."* (Exodus 7:22)

Strike two.

2.   Second, God brought a plague of frogs upon Egypt. (Exodus 8:1-15). *"The Nile will teem with frogs. They will come up into your palace and your bedroom and onto your bed, into the houses of your officials and on your people, and into your ovens and kneading troughs. The frogs will come up on you and your people and all your officials.' "* (Exodus 8:3-4)

And it happened just that way. But again, the royal magicians of Egypt were able to duplicate this miracle. Whether it was by illusion or by Satanic power that they were able to do this, we are never told.

Nevertheless, Pharaoh agreed to let the people of God leave Egypt if only Moses would alleviate the plague. Moses prayed for relief from the plague at a time specified by Pharaoh and the frogs all died. Although they stank! (Can you imagine dead frogs everywhere--in your bed and in your ovens and kitchen bowls?)

But, true to form, *"when Pharaoh saw that there was relief, he hardened his heart and would not listen to Moses and Aaron, just as the LORD had said."* (Exodus 8:15)

Strike three.

I am not going to elaborate on each plague but for the next several it states that Pharaoh hardened his heart. He decided of his own volition that he would not let the Hebrews go.

3.   Plague of Gnats (8.16-19)

Exodus 8:19: *"Pharaoh's heart was hard and he would not listen."*

Strike four.

4.   Plague of Flies (8.20-32)

Exodus 8.32 *"Pharaoh's hardened his heart"*

Strike five

5.   Plague of Death of all Egyptian Livestock (9.1-7)

Exodus 9.7 *"Pharaoh's heart was unyielding and he would not let the people go."*

Strike six. (are you beginning to see a pattern here?)

6.   Plague of Boils (9.8-12)

Exodus 9.12 *"The Lord hardened Pharaoh's heart and he would not listen to Moses and Aaron, just as the Lord had said to Moses."*

7.   Plague of Hail (9.13-35)

Exodus 9.34 *"Pharaoh and his officials hardened their hearts."*

Strike seven.

In baseball, it is "Three strikes and you're out!" In the case of Pharaoh, God was more gracious. It was "Strike seven!" before God said "You're out!"(excluding the exception of #6: the Plague of Boils).

After seven chances to change his mind, the wording changes. God is done waiting. Now He will not allow Pharaoh to repent or change his mind. God says,

> *Go to Pharaoh, for I have hardened his heart and the hearts of his officials so that I may perform these signs of mine among them that you may tell your children and grandchildren how I dealt harshly with the Egyptians and how I performed my signs among them, and that you may know that I am the LORD. (Exodus 10:1-2).*

Pharaoh's hard heart was now irrevocably cast and each plague became a prelude to final judgment. (This is a cautionary tale to me of times when I harden my heart. Will the point come at which I have hardened my heart enough times that God will solidify my hardened heart so that I cannot repent in order that the full consequences of sin may be seen in my life?)[35] *(For a response to a objection to this line of comparison, see the endnote).*

8.   Plague of Locusts (10.1-20)

Exodus 10.20 *"The Lord hardened Pharaoh's heart."*

9.   Plague of Darkness (10.21-29)

Exodus 10.27 *"The Lord hardened Pharaoh's heart."*

10. Plague of Death of the Firstborn

Exodus 11.10 *"The Lord hardened Pharaoh's heart."*

Any chances at repentance were done. For the first seven plagues it says that God gave Pharaoh the opportunity to repent. After the seventh, Pharaoh no longer had that option. God hardened his heart so that he could not repent.

After the Hebrews had left Egypt, Pharaoh did repent—but he repented of ever letting them go in the first place! But God said to Moses, *"I will harden Pharaoh's heart and he will pursue them,"* (Exodus 14:4, 8)

And when the Egyptian army came to the dry bed of the Red Sea while the waters were being held back, God hardened Pharaoh's heart one last time: *"I will harden the hearts of the Egyptians so that they will go in after them."* (Exodus 14:17)

The hardening by God continued up until the fateful destruction of Pharaoh and his army as the Red Sea came crashing down upon them.

That "inner self, the hidden core of being" can be hardened by disobedience, disappointments, and it's most extreme manifestation, despair.

Prov. 13:12 says, *"Hope deferred makes the heart sick."*

This hardheartedness results in an inability to see hope in Christ. There is no hope in the future, or in anything and any evidence to the contrary is dismissed.

In *Pilgrim's Progress*, John Bunyan has the protagonist "Christian" being led into a dark room where a man is imprisoned in an iron cage. His eyes are downcast, "he sat with his eyes looking down to the ground, his hands folded together, and he sighed as if he would break his heart."

Christian begins to question the man and finds that he was at once "a fair and flourishing professor, [of faith in Christ] both in [his] own eyes, and also in the eyes of others."

But, the man says, he has sinned so grievously that he believes he cannot repent.

When Christian reminds the man in the iron cage of the mercy of God, and urges him to "repent and turn" the man replies, "God hath denied me repentance. His word gives me no encouragement to believe; yea, himself hath shut me up in this iron cage: nor can all the men in the world let me out. Oh eternity! eternity! how shall I grapple with the misery that I must meet with in eternity?[36]

Many today suffer from despair. Henri Nouwen says that "We are…deeply affected by life's disappointments and setbacks. They remind us that, sooner or later, everything decays. Despair is our inner conviction that, in the end, it is utterly impossible to stop anything from coming to nothing."[37]

The cause of this despair can vary, but ultimately it comes down to a refusal to believe in the goodness and power of God. One might say that this is hardheartedness caused by sin, such as was Pharaoh's, but this seems different. It is not hardheartedness arising from pride, but hardheartedness coming from despair.

What are the results of hardheartedness? First, unteachableness: an inability or unwillingness to perceive and understand. In addition the person with a hard heart is often unsympathetic to the needs of others, and if the hard heart comes from disobedience it usually results in continued disobedience. (Disobedience is both evidence of and cause of a hard heart.)

What is the cure for hardheartedness? The main cure is repentance.

Repentance is both an attitude as well as a behavior. It is literally a "change of heart." Do you remember how the *Dictionary of Bible Themes* defined "heart"? "The total inner self, a person's hidden core of being."[38]

Repentance is not primarily "feeling bad". It means that my total inner self--who I am at my essence--changes in mind, will and actions so that I begin to think, desire and behave differently.

Where before acts of neglect toward God and things concerning Him led to habits of neglect, now I begin to practice acts of obedience and worship toward God.

Where before, repeated acts of disregard toward other people, led to a habit of disregard, now I begin to seek to find ways to show love and compassion towards other people.

Where before, a disregard of God's Word and commandments led to disobedience, now my focus becomes on attention and obedience to His Word.

Where before, I blinded myself to others' feelings; saying and doing everyday things which wound them, till at last I become unconscious of their very existence, and think nothing real which is not, in some manner, my own. Now I begin to pay attention to those who are around me, listen to them and begin to treat them with attention and care.

The two hands of attitude and action must go together to cure hardheartedness. Simple blind action, without any reflection and change of heart will not ultimately succeed. But simple attitude change (or, *supposed* attitude change) without action also will never result in the softening of a hard heart

Success and Demonstrated Talent

As ironic as it may seem, (or maybe not) a huge stumbling block to our teachableness is our own success and talents. The young salmon in the fable preceding this chapter had to learn that. Most talented people have difficulties when it comes to staying teachable. They have reached a level of success or acclaim doing what they do best. They are surrounded by people who praise them and tell them how wonderful they are (or at least, how wonderful is their performance). The temptation is to believe that they know it all. That makes it hard for them to keep developing. Teachability is not so much about competence and mental capacity as it is about attitude: it's the hunger to discover and grow.

One of the most profound observations about hindrances to teachableness for me personally came from Brian Houston, senior pastor of Hillsong Church, based out of Australia. In a teaching on "Having a Teachable Spirit,"[39] Houston looked at the story of Jesus and the Rich Young Ruler. (Mark 10:17-31)

The Rich Young Ruler came to Jesus, appearing as if he had a very teachable spirit. *"As Jesus started on his way, a man ran up to him and fell on his knees before him. 'Good teacher,' he asked, 'what must I do to inherit eternal life?'"* (Mark 10:17). You don't get it more served up on a silver platter than that!

The young man thought that Jesus was lobbing the softball he had lobbed to Jesus back to him: *"You know the commandments: 'You shall not murder, you shall not commit adultery, you shall not steal, you shall not give false testimony, you shall not defraud, honor your father and mother.'"* (10:19)

I picture the young man probably standing a little bit taller and smiling as he said: *"'Teacher,' he declared, 'all these I have kept since I was a boy.'"* (10:20)

The beautiful thing is that for most of us that would be an untrue exaggeration of our own moral goodness. But that was not the case with this man. Mark records that *"Jesus looked at him and loved him."* (10:21a)

But then came the bombshell: *"One thing you lack,"* he said. *"Go, sell everything you have and give to the poor, and you will have treasure in heaven. Then come, follow me."*

As Brian Houston notes, Jesus was telling the young man:

1. Don't come follow me until you have taken care of your own issues. There are still things you need to address.

2. Your problem is that you don't own your possessions, your possessions own you. "Sell everything"

3. You need to learn generosity. Give the money to the poor.

4. Decide you want to live for kingdom purposes, and you will have treasure in heaven.

But some of the saddest words in the Bible (at least for me) are *"At this the man's face fell. He went away sad, because he had great wealth."*

The young man had so much: moral excellence, position (Luke says that he was "a ruler"), wealth and at least some level of spiritual interest. We would think that would be enough! But the question for Jesus, was: "Was he teachable?"

The very strengths, success and demonstrated talent that he possessed were the things that kept him from being teachable about the things that really mattered.

Success and demonstrated talent are marvelous gifts from God. But without discernment and teachableness, they can be destructive.

When I was young, I learned the principle (put colloquially) "Dance with the one what brung ya." That means stick with the thing that brought you to where you are today. But new circumstances can demand new methods or new ways of thinking. If we are chained to the ways that brought us success in the past, we will not be successful in the new endeavor.

Success can lead us to count success by the wrong criteria. A church may grow to huge numbers of people in attendance, but men and women are not being made into disciples of Jesus.

A job may lead to higher pay, shorter hours, more leisure and financial independence, but not be the job for which God fashioned us.

Broadcaster Paul Harvey was famous for his "The Rest of the Story" accounts. Several years ago he told the following story illustrating that a man exhibiting great talent in one are did not experience automatic success when he applied those principles in another area:

> There was an old man who was a great admirer of democracy and public education. So close to his heart did he hold both institutions that he tried to bring them together into one grand experiment, a public college where students would practice self-governance. There would be no regulations; the goodwill and judgment of the students would suffice. After years of planning, the school was finally opened. The old man was overjoyed.
>
> But as the months went by, students proved time and time again that they were not the models of discipline and discernment the old man envisioned. They skipped classes, drank to excess, and wasted hours in frivolous pursuits. One night, 14 students, disguised by masks and "animated with wine," went on a rampage that ended in a brawl. One struck a professor with a brick, and another used a cane on his victim.
>
> In response, the college's trustees convened a special meeting. The old man, now 82 years old and very frail, was asked to address the student body. In his remarks, he recalled the lofty principles upon which the college had been founded. He said he had expected more—much more—from the students. He even confessed that this was the most painful event of his life. Suddenly, he stopped speaking. Tears welled up in his failing eyes. He was so overcome with grief that he sat down, unable to go on.
>
> His audience was so touched that at the conclusion of the meeting the 14 offenders stepped forward to admit their guilt.

But they could not undo the damage already done. A strict code of conduct and numerous onerous regulations were instituted at the college. The old man's experiment had failed. Why? Because he took for granted the one essential ingredient necessary for success: virtue. Only a virtuous people can secure and maintain their freedom.

A short time later, on the Fourth of July, the old man passed away. Engraved on his tombstone were the simple words that reflected the success and failure of his most important experiments: "Thomas Jefferson, author of the Declaration of Independence and father of the University of Virginia." Now…you know the rest of the story.[40]

Great success can blind us to certain truths and make us unteachable. A good rule of thumb is to ask, "What is success doing to my character, personality and disposition?" Success doesn't MAKE anything happen. It reveals what is already in one's heart.

An Insistence on Understanding

One hindrance to teachableness may make us extremely uncomfortable. At least it has made me uncomfortable. The ironic thing is that most parents encounter this hindrance in their five year old children.

We, at least as Americans, are fascinated with understanding. We want to understand how things work, whether it is a diesel engine or world economic influences. To be told that we need to wait to understand something makes many of us very agitated. It especially agitates us when we are told that we cannot understand something until we have more experience.

I ran across this idea in an odd place. I was browsing through an old volume: *The Philosophical, Theological and Miscellaneous Works of the*

Rev. William Jones, published in 1801 and saw a chapter on Teachableness. (volume 11, pages 209-216).

Rev. Jones refers to the military and its training. Many times soldiers are taught skills for which they don't see the use. It is only in battle that they see the purpose of the skills they had been taught. Jones says,

> The soldier...submits to learn things of which he does not see the use. And is not every learner under the same obligation? If he desires to be taught, must not he bring with him that teachable disposition, which receives the rules and elements of learning implicitly, and trusts to the future for the knowledge of those reasons on which they are grounded? This is not a matter of choice: he can be taught on no other principle; for though the practice of a rule may seem very easy, the reason of that rule will generally lie too deep for a beginner; and long experience will be necessary before it can be understood: indeed there are many rules established, for which we have no reason but experience.[41]

What parent has not said to her five year old (or similarly aged) child when asked incessantly, "Why?" "Because I say so!!" The parent knows that the child is totally unable to comprehend the reason for the rule or restriction. No amount of reasoning will convince the child because the child does not have the experience, reasoning ability or knowledge base to come to an understanding of the reasons.

No amount of reasoning will convince the child that he should not touch the hot stove. He must simply obey. Eventually, he will come to understand the reasons for the warning, but the child must learn to conform his behavior long before he can understand why.

The child must obey the rule not to run into the street, whether or not she understands why. A parent can explain, but the child is incapable of the reasoning necessary, "But I will see the car and be able to get out of the way!" "But if I don't run into the street after the ball, it may be lost or get hit itself." She or he is not capable of understanding the damage that a moving vehicle can do to a little girl or boy.

And yet how many of us are like that five year old. Unless we can understand the reason behind a principle or truth, we balk at adopting it. Most of us have known (or have been!) someone who "had to learn everything the hard way." Why? Because he or she refused to accept a rule or restriction unless they understood the reason behind it. And yet, they were often experientially unable to understand the reason! And so, eventually after (usually bruising) experience, they come to adapt to the truth—whether or not they fully understand it. But time has been wasted. Opportunities have been lost. Perhaps bad habits have been adopted that make a new way of living much more difficult, if not impossible. Jones words it: "he will contract bad habits in the beginning and perhaps find himself unfit to be taught, when he would be glad to learn."[42]

This fault is characteristic of many youth, although not exclusively. At its core, it is a combination of pride and insecurity:

• **Pride** in that I presume that if something is explained to me, I will be able to understand it. The serpent appealed to this in Eve. She did not understand WHY God had said not to eat of the fruit. And so Satan appealed to her pride, *"God knows that when you eat of it your eyes will be opened, and you will be like God, knowing good and evil."* (Gen. 3:5 ESV) Satan lies: God wants to keep something from you that is rightfully yours: the knowledge of good and evil. You DESERVE to know that. Take and eat.

• **Insecurity** in that I don't trust the person who is asking me to do something a certain way, even though I don't understand it. Perhaps we have been deceived before and so, in our suspicious fear of being deceived again, we refuse to commit until we understand. In business transactions this is usually a good characteristic: we don't buy or invest until we understand as much as we can. But in life learning, which is much bigger than where we invest our money or the toaster we buy, that same idea can backfire and cause us grievous harm.

OR, we don't trust ourselves. We may not believe that we have the ability to understand a concept, or to change our behavior or to accomplish a goal. Why try to learn when, we believe down deep that we cannot learn?

For the first few years of my coaching business, I would make a statement that undercut my teachableness. I would say, "I am not good at marketing." In order for your business to be known and attract clients, there are certain actions that you need to do. The actions vary, but the fact that action is required is true in all businesses and endeavors.

My business didn't grow very fast outside my immediate circle of friends and people over whom I had influence. I did a few marketing things and they did not seem to be all that productive.

My vision of a marketer was of a slick snake-oil salesman (although I've never met a literal snake-oil salesman and snake-oil sales seem to have plummeted long before I was born!).

But the statement, "I am not good at marketing" had several deleterious effects:

a.   I could blame any failure at business on my "inability to market" effectively.

b.   There was no reason for me to improve at marketing because "I was not good" at it! (That is false logic, but the logic I employed none the less).

c.   I would read an occasional marketing book or attend an occasional marketing workshop, but went in with the attitude that this may work for some people, but it won't work for me. The attitude I took in made me unteachable.

d.   I didn't have strong motivation to improve as a marketer because I had false ideas about what marketing entailed.

My insecurities about lack of business success and lack of marketing success, led me to the conclusion that I don't understand enough about marketing and so I am a bad marketer, made me unteachable (at least for a while).

Being teachable is not necessarily our default mode. Pride, fear, laziness, complaining and criticizing, sins deceitfulness, callousness/a hard heart/obduracy, success and demonstrated talent, and an insistence on understanding are just some of the hindrances that can keep us from being teachable.

Chapter Four: Questions for Personal Thought and Group Discussion

Eight possible reasons for a lack of teachableness are mentioned.

Pride

- Why do you think that pride is listed as the core of many of the other reasons for unteachableness? Can you give an example in your own life?

Fear

- What thing(s) do you fear today that may be keeping you from learning a needed lesson today?

Laziness

- In what ways does being teachableness demand hard work?

Complaining & Criticizing

- Do a heart check. Are you a complainer or critic? Of what has that robbed you in your life?

Sin's Deceitfulness

- In what ways is sin in your life today making you resistant to teachableness?

Callousness/A Hard Heart

- Of what do you need to repent in order to allow your heart to begin to soften?

Success and Demonstrated Talent

- Were you surprised that this cause of unteachableness was included? Why? Have you seen examples of this in your own experience?

An Insistence on Understanding

- Are there things in your life now that you are failing to do because you are waiting on being able to understand? What part do fear and insecurity play in that for you?

Fable #5: The Tortoise and the Ducks

"Take me with you, please," called a tortoise to a gray duck and a white duck that were flying over.

The ducks heard the tortoise and flew down toward him.

"Do you really wish to go with us?" asked the ducks as they came to the ground near the tortoise.

"I surely do," replied the tortoise. "Will you please take me?"

"Why, yes, I think we can do so," said the white duck slowly.

The two ducks talked together in low tones for a few minutes. Then they flew to the woods. They soon brought back a strong twig and dropped it in front of the tortoise.

"Now," said the ducks, "if we take you off to see the world, you must promise us one thing."

"What is that?" asked the tortoise. "I will promise almost anything if you will let me go."

"Because you will be holding on to the stick with your mouth and jaw, you must promise not to say one word while you are in the air, NOT ONE WORD," replied the ducks.

"All right, I promise," said the tortoise. "Sometimes I do not say a word for a whole day because there is no one to listen to me."

"Well, take firm hold of the middle of the twig with your mouth; we are ready to start," said the gray duck.

"If you value your life, you must hold on tightly," said the white duck.

The tortoise took hold of the middle of the twig with his mouth and each duck took hold of one end.

Then they flew up! up! up! while the tortoise swung from the middle of the twig. How he enjoyed it! He had never had such a ride.

They had gone a long way safely when they came to a hayfield. The haymakers looked up and saw the ducks and the tortoise.

"Ho! ho! the tortoise has stolen some wings," called one of the haymakers.

"What a queer carriage he has!" laughed another in a loud voice.

"I pity his horses," said another.

This made the tortoise so angry that he opened his mouth and cried out, "You—" but no one knows what he was going to say, for at once he fell–splat—to the ground.[43]

Moral-The failure to follow wise words can lead to heartache.

CHAPTER 5: PRECEPTS AND PRINCIPLES.
How Does God Teach? Part 1

Dear Lord Jesus, Help me not just to read the Bible but to have the Bible constantly reading me—exposing my sin and brokenness and revealing more and more and more of the riches of the gospel.[44]

--Scotty Smith
Founding Pastor of Christ Community Church, Franklin, TN

Daniel had been sitting at the coffee shop for two hours now, staring out the window at the bleak winter day. The harsh winds rattled the closed canopies that in warmer weather would be shading laughing couples from the sun. The trees were all barren. No leaves clung to the dry empty branches; each branch pointed up to heaven as each one was appealing to God for spring and new life.

Daniel's soul was as barren as the trees. His grande coffee cup was long since empty and he had folded the coffee cup sleeve into almost every imaginable shape. There was no reasonable excuse for staying at the table any longer than he had.

No reason except that he was avoiding going home.

He knew what he faced there.

Nothing.

Nothing in all of its heaviness.

Brenda would have been home and gone by now. As she had shouted at him and then slammed the door, she said she would be returning this morning to get clothes and makeup and other personal things. He was not to dare be there when she came back. And he hadn't been.

He had no idea where she had gone last night. To her friend Sandy's, perhaps. Maybe to her boss Davina's house. Probably not to her mother's house. Checking their personal credit card accounts at work, it didn't appear that she had checked into a hotel.

But what was certain is that when he got home…she would have come and gone. There would be nothing of her there. Perhaps a scent of her in her dressing area. Perhaps the engagement picture, that had hung in their bedroom since right after the wedding, would still be there. He doubted if she would have taken that. But Brenda, her essence, would be gone.

Why hadn't he done anything sooner? After his own father had left his mother he swore that he would never have a marriage fall apart. Fortunately there were no kids to be affected as he had been, but he had pledged to Brenda over and over that their marriage was a forever marriage. Why had he repeated the same mistakes that his parents had made? He knew them as he made them. The checks written with no money to cover them. Occasionally getting caught looking at pornography on his computer. He hadn't physically committed adultery like his father, but he had done it a thousand times in his mind. For some reason, the words, the cynicism, the silences seemed to flow out of him without him even thinking.

Probably that was part of the problem…not thinking.

Just this past Sunday, their pastor had preached on Ephesians 5:

Husbands, love your wives, just as Christ loved the church and gave himself up for her to make her holy, cleansing[b] her by the washing with water through the word, and to present her to himself as a radiant church, without stain or wrinkle or any other blemish, but holy and blameless. In this same way, husbands ought to love their wives as their own bodies. He who loves his wife loves himself. After all, no one ever hated their own body, but they feed and care for their body, just as Christ does the church—for we are members of his body. "For this reason a man will leave his father and mother and be united to his wife, and the two will become one flesh." (Ephesians 5:25-31)

They had sat side by side, Daniel and Brenda, fit and neatly dressed. Smiling and greeting those around them warmly. Had anyone noticed how they had both leaned away from one another as the preacher preached? Brenda couldn't elbow him when the words from Eph. 5 were read because her arms were tightly folded across her chest. He was glad he didn't know what was going on in her head during that sermon.

He had heard those words from the Bible a hundred (or more) times before. He probably could have quoted them along with Pastor Jeff as he read them.

He remembered thinking, "Well, I don't live up to that, but who really does?" The apostle Paul was single and he especially wasn't married to Brenda! He really had no idea…".

Little did he know that by Thursday those words would be coming back to him as a prophecy of doom. He hadn't taken the words all that seriously until now. Why hadn't he listened and implemented even a few things about each one in their marriage?

And now, he was starting a new journey. He really didn't expect Brenda to come back. He had refused to go to marriage counseling for so long, she had given up asking.

Did he even WANT her to come back? He thought and realized he didn't know what he wanted. He had felt so very little for so long. He certainly didn't want the fighting to return. He didn't want the days where they communicated through soliloquies of silence.

Why did he have to learn everything the hard way? The new journey was about to begin.

He needed to let his parents know. He would call them tonight. At least there would be one or two human voices in the house tonight, even if they only came through the phone.

Daniel rolled the cup sleeve into a tight roll and stuffed it through the drink opening on the plastic lid on his cup. He stood and dropped the cup in the trash can as he moved slowly toward the door.

It was time. It was time to go home.

———————

A while ago, I put up a question on my Facebook page: "What ways has God used to teach you something that he wants you to learn?"

The responses were both touching and sobering in their honesty:

- "A broken heart (He definitely used that)."
- "By humbling me."
- "Abandonment. I learned that He is sufficient to meet my needs."
- "A perfectly timed book"
- "Children, esp. those who aren't 'typical.'"
- "Pursuing me until I obey!"
- "Real miracles for a life that seemed to go 'wrong.' But different answers than what I wanted. I had to see it to understand it."
- "Showing me something in the garden"
- "Having no job and no friends in a new place of residence...loss of job"
- "Heartaches from adult children"
- "His Word...Promises in His Word"
- "I remember taking biology at _____ University and thinking about the incredible creativity God possess. Nothing would be impossible for one who can pack so much life into little bitty seeds."

These answers were given by just a small number of my Facebook friends who saw the post and chose to respond within a 24 hour period. The ways that God teaches are vast...and often uncomfortable.

Just as it is difficult or impossible to describe all of the lessons that God wants to teach us, so it is difficult to describe all the ways that he teaches. Like the specific lessons, the ways may be as numerous as the people who need to be taught.

However God teaches, there seem to be three categories that are helpful to understand: the easiest ways to receive God's lessons, the more challenging ways to receive God's lessons, and the hardest ways to receive God's lessons. We'll look at those three ways in this and the following two chapters and each will relate to my story of Daniel's reflection at the coffee shop.

Study Precepts and Principles

The first way that God teaches us (and the way most of us wish we could learn things) is through godly precepts and principles. "Precept" comes from the Latin word *praeceptum*: "command or order." *The Oxford Pocket Dictionary* defines it as "a general rule intended to regulate behavior or thought."[45]

A cultural precept can be as common as

- "Two wrongs don't make a right."

- "Hope for the best, but prepare for the worst."

- "Fortune favors the bold."

- "Keep your friends close and your enemies closer."

The Oxford Pocket Dictionary defines "principles" as "a fundamental truth or proposition that serves as the foundation for a system of belief or behavior or for a chain of reasoning"[46]

For those of us for whom the Bible is the supreme authoritative source, it is filled with both precepts and principles. What is the difference? Dr. David Reid gives an excellent differentiation in using the difference between Exodus 20:13 and Acts 1:8:

- Exodus: 20:13: *"You shall not murder."*

- Acts 1:8: *"But you will receive power when the Holy Spirit has come upon you, and you will be my witnesses in Jerusalem and in all Judea and Samaria, and to the end of the earth."*

Ex. 20:13 is a precept: a command that is to be followed. Simple as that.

Acts 1:8 contains a principle: a command that is to be followed, but usually does not need to be followed in the literal way that it is stated. (i.e. not everyone needs personally to go to Jerusalem, Judea, Samaria and to the end of the earth to be obedient to the principle that Christ here commands.)

Dr. Reid draws at least three conclusions from the principles in Acts 1:8:

1. The power of the Holy Spirit is essential for effective evangelism.

2. Potential foreign missionaries should start evangelizing right where they are, before setting off for a foreign mission field.

3. It's good missionary strategy to evangelize the big cities first, so the gospel can ripple out to the countryside.[47]

Learning from precepts and principles is different from learning from the examples around us. The examples usually present one life lesson each. There is an overriding theme or lesson to the story. You get it or you don't. It takes more effort to search out the precepts and principles of life and of the Bible. It takes discernment: is this a precept or a principle. If so, how does that apply to my life situation?

One stated purpose of the Bible is to teach the teachable:

All Scripture is God-breathed and is useful for teaching, rebuking, correcting and training in righteousness, so that the servant of God may be thoroughly equipped for every good work. (2 Timothy 3.16-17)

The truth is that there is a lot to learn in life—some of it temporal and some of it eternal. We spend an amazing amount of time learning the things that will equip us to live on this temporal earth. And (for the most part) there is nothing wrong with that.

But how much time do we spend learning the things that equip us to live as eternal beings now and into the future? If we are going to be *"thoroughly equipped for every good work"* it is critical that we learn from Scripture.

The classic example of learning from precept is the study of the Old Testament book of Proverbs. I call it "A Handbook for the Teachable".

In fact, that is why the writer says that the book was written: to teach the teachable. The book begins:

The proverbs of Solomon son of David, king of Israel: for gaining wisdom and instruction; for understanding words of insight; for receiving instruction in prudent behavior, doing what is right and just and fair; for giving prudence to those who are simple, knowledge and discretion to the young— let the wise listen and add to their learning, and let the discerning get guidance— for understanding proverbs and parables, the sayings and riddles of the wise. (Proverbs 1:1–6)

Simply look at chapters 1 and 2 [there are other examples in those chapters besides what I note here].

- The correct attitude must be present for us to be teachable (1:7)
- Some people delight in their lack of teachableness (1:22)
- A lack of teachableness can be fatal (1:32)
- Teachableness includes listening to parents (1:8–9; cf. 10:18)
- The invariable result of a lack of teachableness is disaster (1:20–33)
- Teachableness is not easy (2:1-5)
- The results of teachableness (2:6-22)

The Bible is filled with self-claims about the importance and benefits of learning from and studying Scriptures. Psalm 119 lists almost fifty reasons to study and learn from God's Word.[48]

The first and easiest way for us to learn from God is from His precepts and principles. There are dangers in this way of learning (as there are with all ways).

The first danger is that of intellectualism. That is not to say that we should (must) not involve our full intellect in the search for truth from the scriptures and from life.

Dictionary.com defines "intellectualism" as:

1. devotion to intellectual pursuits.

2. the exercise of the intellect.

3. excessive emphasis on abstract or intellectual matters, especially with a lack of proper consideration for emotions.

It is that third meaning of the word that I am using when I talk about the danger of intellectualism. An "excessive emphasis on abstract or intellectual matters, especially with a lack of proper consideration for emotions." (While I might add "without a proper consideration for emotion or spiritual insight", I can actually live with the definition as given).

The reasons for intellectualism may vary. The chief reason, in my opinion, is an unwillingness to deal with the consequences of the teaching. It is "safer" to just go to an intellectual place of understanding and be able to avoid application, or living out the truth.

I know that in my own life, Bible college and seminary were some of the more spiritually dry times in my life. That was not necessarily a problem unique to the specific college or seminaries I attended. I have heard the same both from students at other colleges and seminaries, as well as from elders in the local church. (Although spiritual formation was totally unacknowledged back then in the academic institutions I attended, later [to their credit] they have been added.) Numerous (former) elders have also described their time of service as "the most spiritually dry time" of their lives.

Studying the Bible through the eyes of history, language and literature should enhance, not detract from a devotion to the God of the Bible. In many cases it became a dry intellectual exercise. It was easy to divorce the practical implications of the scriptures from what we were studying. In fact, one of my prominent professors bragged about that: "We will NOT teach you how to apply the things you learn here at _____ school." The stated reason was that changing times demand changing applications. "If we teach you methods of application, they will become obsolete in 10 or 20 years. If we give you a solid foundation in theory and study of the Bible and theology, you should be able to apply these principles to actual life and ministry for yourselves."

While I see the point that the instructor was making, the reality is that if we don't have experience in applying those theories and principles to the time at which they are taught, we are much less likely to correctly apply them to upcoming times.

But most damaging is that this attitude tends to help us see the Bible as only a historical or religious document to be studied academically.

In Matthew 23:13-36 (as well as other places) Jesus condemned the scribes and Pharisees for their intellectualized approach to applying the Bible. They could justify doing whatever they wanted to do by appealing to scripture, while at the same time violating its spirit and principles.

A second danger in learning from the Bible is thinking that because the Bible contains God's truth, that by knowing the Bible, we have come to the highest and deepest knowledge and understanding of what it says. By making our current understanding of biblical truth the complete and final way in which it can be understood, we show a great deal of self-centered pride.

Almost all Christians have had the experience of reading a passage of scripture that they have read or heard before, but this time seeing in it something that is totally new. Was that not there before? Of course it was.

A classically tragic example of this is the attitude of the church for many centuries towards human slavery. While the church was a driver behind the abolition of slavery, that was not always the attitude of the church.

Henry G. Brinton, author of "Balancing Acts: Obligation, Liberation, and Contemporary Christian Conflicts" says in a 2011 USA Today article:

> In the 1860s, Southern preachers defending slavery also took the Bible literally. They asked who could question the Word of God when it said, *"slaves, obey your earthly masters with fear and trembling"* (Ephesians 6:5), or *"tell slaves to be submissive to their masters and to give satisfaction in every respect"* (Titus 2:9).[49]

In time (and with a Civil War, at least in the US) the church came to understand these passages in a new way. Had the texts of scripture changed? No. Did the church now come to doubt the inspired nature of these verses? Again, no. It was that a new understanding came to be held church wide toward these passages.

What am I saying? Only that it is important to hold our understandings of scriptural passages both tightly and lightly at the same time. That may sound contradictory, but I don't believe it is. We hold firmly to the things that we understand God has taught us through scripture.

On the other hand, we always recognize that none of us are all-knowing and infallible. Our interpretations of scripture must be able to be adapted as God's Spirit continues to work to refine his church through the millennia.

I had coffee recently with a very good friend. He is a godly man who came to faith as an adult and has continued to grow and develop in his faith. He is currently taking classes at a seminary here in Portland while he continues his job with a large health care corporation. He's not sure how he will use his education… that's up to God, but he knows that he needs to learn.

He came to the coffee shop directly from the seminary and was in an excited state. He could hardly wait to tell me some of things he had learned: "Justice is mentioned more than 2,000 times in the Bible. That is twice as many times as 'love' or 'heaven' -- and seven times more often than 'hell'."

Sam kept saying, "This is just blowing my mind. It is not only challenging my understanding, but it is challenging my political beliefs as well!"

I smiled, because I knew that my friend was an example of a teachable person…and God was in the process of taking him into new places by teaching him from the precepts and principles of His Word.

Chapter 5: Questions for Personal Thought and Group Discussion

- What ways has God used to teach you something that he wants you to learn?

- How long has it been since you read the book of Proverbs? This time of studying teachableness may be a good opportunity to do that!

- When have you seen intellectualism stunt the power of God's Word in your life? In the life of others?

- What can you do to fight intellectualism in your daily life? If you are a leader, how can you fight intellectualism in your life while serving in leadership?

- What is a scripture of which you have come to a new understanding recently? Did that call you to action? If so, what action did you take?

Fable #6: The Crab and His Mother

"Why in the world do you walk sideways like that?" said a son crab to his mother. "You should always walk straight forward with your toes turned out."

"Show me how to walk, dear son," answered the mother crab with a smile, "I want to learn."

So the young crab tried and tried to walk straight forward. But he could walk sideways only, like his mother. And when he wanted to turn his toes out he tripped and fell on his nose.

Finally the young crab gave up and began walking as his mother (and all crabs) do.[50]

Moral: We are wise to follow the example of others.

CHAPTER 6: THE EXAMPLES OF OTHERS.
How Does God Teach? Part 2

Learn from the mistakes of others. You can't live long enough to make them all yourself."

-- attributed to everyone from ancient Indian philosopher Chanakya (or Vishnu Gupta), to jurist Oliver Wendell Holmes and to first lady Eleanor Roosevelt

Another way that God teaches us is through the example of others. That is one of the advantages of studying the lives of others, whether in the Bible or in biographies or in history. The statement with which I begin this chapter has been attributed to many people, but it is true no matter who first said it.

My wife and her brother who is eighteen months younger than her have an inside joke between them: She got in trouble often as a young girl (she was like the first brother in Jesus parable of the two sons in Luke 21:28-32—she balked but eventually complied). Her brother, on the other hand did (he says) many more things of which his parents would have disapproved –if they had known about them. But he had learned from his older sister's example what not to say and what not to do to keep their parents from finding out.

If we are wise we will learn from the example of others—both good and bad. What went well for others and what did not go well for others…and why.

Now, while that is a negative example of learning from others, there are manifold opportunities to learn positive things from the example of others.

The Bible is a book full of stories.[51] We have stories from the lives of literally hundreds of men and women who lived over at least a 2,000 year period of time. No one, apart from Jesus Christ in the New Testament, is depicted as faultless. From Eve's acquiescing to the serpent's temptation…all the way down to the apostle Peter having to be chastised by Paul because he shunned non-Jewish Christians when Jewish Christians came around. No one was faultless.

Chart A: Deciphering the Learnable Lessons from a Person's Life

a. Name of Person

b. Verses in the Bible where that person is found

c. What Character Traits (positive or negative) do you see in their life? How was that exhibited?

d. What were the consequences of his or her behavior?

e. How did God show grace to this person?

f. What Bible truths/scriptures are illustrated (positively or negatively) in this person's life?

g. Lesson learned from this person/these persons:

h. What do I need to do in response to this life lesson?

i. Lessons to be Learned

j. Questions/Notes

I gauge this method to be a little bit harder than learning from Biblical precept and principle because where most of the commands and precepts are pretty straightforward, when you look at the example of someone in the Bible, you often must decipher: what is the lesson to be learned from this individual.

I have a homemade tool that I use to help decipher the lessons from biblical people's lives. (See Chart A, above)

An example of how I might fill this out would be found in Chart B. (below)

Now the example of Adam and Eve on my second chart may or may not be helpful to you or provocative for you, but having some little tool in mind, or by your side to help you can help you better mine the riches of someone else's experience.

In his last known letter, the apostle Paul gives us a great glimpse into the idea of what it means to learn from the example of others.

Chart B: Deciphering the Learnable Lessons from the Lives of Adam and Eve

a. Name: Adam and Eve

b. Verses in the Bible where that person is found (Gen. 1-3)

c. What Character Traits (positive or negative) do you see in their life? How was that exhibited?
Disobeying God and eating of the fruit of the tree of the knowledge of good and evil.

d. What were the consequences of their behavior?
   i. They would physically die.
   ii. They were banished from the Garden. (particularly from the Tree of Life) (3:23-24)
   iii. Men would have to toil to get food from the ground. (3:17-19)
   iv. Women would suffer in childbirth. (3:16)
   v. They knew the pain of one son killing the other. (ch. 4:9-22)
   vi. Adam lived 930 years before he died. (Gen. 5.5)

e. How did God show grace to this person?
   i. Even while passing judgment on Adam and Eve, God gave the promise of the coming Messiah. (Even in one of history's darkest sins, God brought/promised redemption)
   ii. God gave Adam and Eve Seth to replace Abel. (plus many other sons and daughters) (4:25)

Lessons from Adam and Eve (cont.)

f. **What Bible truths/scriptures are illustrated (positively or negatively) in this person's life?**

    i.   I Cor. 15:33: "Do not be misled, 'Bad company corrupts good character.'" Eve was receptive to being in conversation with the enemy of God.

    ii. Adam was willing to be duped by Eve into believing the serpent's lie.

g. **Lesson learned from this person/these persons:**

    i.   There are consequences to actions.

    ii. We battle a deceiver.

    iii. Sin cannot exist in the presence of God. Ultimately sinful people in his presence will be destroyed.

    iv. Sin has familial consequences (at least learned this after Cain and Abel).

h. **What do I need to do in response to this life lesson?**

    i.   I need to look for the subtle ways Satan seeks to deceive me.

    ii. Half-truths are just as damaging as full lies.

i. **Questions/Notes:** While Moses, Abraham and Elijah are described in the New Testament as being in heaven, it is never said that Adam and Eve are there. Any reason for that?

He has run the course of his life and has been an example for Timothy for decades. He says,

"You, however, know all about my teaching, my way of life, my purpose, faith, patience, love, endurance, persecutions, sufferings—what kinds of things happened to me in Antioch, Iconium and Lystra, the persecutions I endured. Yet the Lord rescued me from all of them. (2 Tim. 3:10–11)

There are wonderful examples of those who were teachable in the Bible:

- David learned from the example of every-day life as he learned to trust God as a shepherd. He even learned from the devastating consequences of his sin with Bathsheba.

- Zechariah, the father of John the Baptist learned about disbelieving God by being struck mute for the duration of his wife's pregnancy.

- Mary of Bethany learned of the power behind Jesus' words, *"I am the resurrection and the life. The one who believes in me will live, even though they die; and whoever lives by believing in me will never die. Do you believe this?"* by seeing her brother, Lazarus, be raised from the dead.

- The crowd on the Day of Pentecost recorded in Acts 2 knew of their need when they cried out in response to Peter's declaration *"Let all the house of Israel therefore know for certain that God has made him both Lord and Christ, this Jesus whom you crucified.' Now when they heard this they were cut to the heart, and said to Peter and the rest of the apostles, 'Brothers, what shall we do?'"* (Acts 2:36–37)

- Paul showed his teachable spirit when he immediately responded to the Words of Christ—the Christ he had been persecuting--after being confronted on the road to Damascus. *"But rise and enter the city, and you will be told what you are to do."* (Acts 9:6).

There are also, however, tragic examples in the Bible of those who refused to be teachable:

- We have already alluded to the rich young ruler, who went away from Christ disappointed because he could not let go of his riches in order to follow Jesus.

- The Pharaoh of Egypt *"became hard and he would not listen to [Moses and Aaron], just as the Lord had said."* (Ex 7:13).

- Many of the religious leaders –especially the scribes and Pharisees--who opposed Jesus demonstrated great unteachableness (Luke 6:6-11; Luke 13:10-17; Matthew 19:8; Matthew 12:38-45; Matthew 16:1-4; Matthew 22:29; Luke 7:36-50).

Naaman is a terrific example of teachableness, both positive and negative. We find the account of Naaman in 2 Kings 5:1-14.

Naaman was the head of the Syrian army (at that point called "Aram"). He was a very successful general and is described as a "mighty warrior." While not of the people of God, the writer of 2 Kings says that God had given victory to Syria/Aram through Naaman's leadership.

Unfortunately, Naaman was a leper. This disease not only limited him and ostracized him from general society, but also would eventually kill him in a very gruesome manner.

Naaman's wife had a servant who was a Hebrew who had been captured and taken prisoner as a young girl. At one point, knowing of Naaman's disease, the servant girl said to her mistress: *"If only my lord were with the prophet who is in Samaria! He would cure him of his leprosy."* (2 Kings 5:3b).

Upon hearing this report, Naaman sent a message to the King of Israel, asking for Elisha's help.

Elisha agreed and sent for Naaman to come to where he was. But instead of seeing him in person, Elisha sent a messenger to where Naaman was staying to say, *""Go, wash in the Jordan seven times, and your flesh shall be restored and you shall be clean."* (5:10b).

Naaman was furious and flatly refused to follow Elisha's instructions: *"I thought that for me he would surely come out, and stand and call on the name of the LORD his God, and would wave his hand over the spot, and cure the leprosy! Are not Abana and Pharpar, the rivers of Damascus, better than all the waters of Israel? Could I not wash in them, and be clean?" He turned and went away in a rage."* (5:11b-12)

Naaman was certainly not teachable. As John Maxwell states in his notes in the *Maxwell Leadership Bible*, Naaman "struggled with pride, faulty expectations, and inflexibility."

Naaman...

1.   ... wanted a quick fix.

2.   ... expected special treatment.

3.   ... held certain assumptions about a solution.

4.   ... grew angry about perceived unfair treatment.

5.   ... rejected the new solution.[52]

But Naaman's example is not completely negative. Naaman showed some teachableness in that that he was smart enough to surround himself with people who were willing to disagree with the general and speak into his life. (Not an easy thing for anyone who serves a very powerful strong minded leader).

But his servants had the courage to speak up. Naaman, likewise had the courage to be teachable. He changed his mind, did what the prophet commanded (still without ever meeting him) and because of his teachableness, Naaman was healed.

Was Jesus Teachable?

Most of us have no problem thinking of David, Zechariah, Mary, the people on the Day of Pentecost, Naaman, Peter, the Ethiopian eunuch, even Paul as being teachable. But Jesus? Was Jesus teachable? If he serves as an example for us in so many ways, is he also an example for us in the area of being teachable?

Most of us react viscerally to any teaching that would say that

Jesus is not morally perfect. (And that is not where I am going). The entire New Testament idea of atonement is based on the spotlessness of the lamb that was shed to take away the sins of the world.

The New Testament is very clear about the moral perfection of Jesus:

> Heb 9:13-14: *"The blood of goats and bulls and the ashes of a heifer sprinkled on those who are ceremonially unclean sanctify them so that they are outwardly clean. How much more, then, will the blood of Christ, who through the eternal Spirit* **offered himself unblemished to God,** *cleanse our consciences from acts that lead to death, so that we may serve the living God!"*

> 2 Corinthians 5:21: *"God made* **him who had no sin** *to be sin for us, so that in him we might become the righteousness of God."*

Any doctrine that would teach that Jesus was not morally perfect is definitely not in the mainstream of historic Christianity.

Moral improvement, however, is not the only area in which we are teachable. The question of whether or not Jesus was teachable gets a little fuzzier when we talk about the omniscience of Jesus. As a general rule we state that Jesus, being God, was all-knowing. It would seem that someone who is all-knowing would not be able to be teachable.

And omniscience is an attribute that some people attribute to Jesus. (Although not all evangelical Christians would require this to be an essential element of Jesus' divinity). There are many things that Jesus knew without learning.

Jesus knew what motivated other people (John 2:24-25), Jesus knew that after his death He was going to be resurrected on the third day and of activities after his resurrection. (John 2:19; Mark 14:28); Jesus knew who was going to betray him. (John 13:11); Jesus knew Peter was going to deny him (John 13:38); Jesus knew that He had come into this world for a short period (Mark 14:7); Jesus knew things of the future (Mark 14:13-16; John 18:4).

But was Jesus all-knowing in EVERY area? In Matthew 24:36 Jesus mentions at least one area in which he is not omniscient: *"But about that day or hour [the Second Coming of the Messiah] no one knows, not even the angels in heaven, nor the Son, but only the Father.*

In addition, it doesn't seem logical that Jesus could never have learned ANYTHING. Did he come out of Mary's womb walking and talking? Did he not have to go to school? Obviously, he did. Luke records: *And as Jesus grew up, he increased in wisdom and in favor with God and people.* (Luke 2:52)

But on a more profound level, Jesus even learned as an adult.

"So Jesus said …I do nothing on my own but speak just what the Father has taught me." (John 8:28b). Apparently even as an adult there were things that Jesus did not know that the Father taught him as Jesus lived. Now, it could be that what Jesus meant was that, while Jesus knew everything, the Father told him WHEN to reveal certain things. But even that knowledge implies that Jesus did not know something: *when* to reveal certain truths.

Charles Spurgeon says of this passage:

Our Great Master never aimed at originality; he said that he did not even speak his own words, but the words that he had heard of his Father. He was docile and teachable; as the Son of God, and the servant of God, his ear was open to hear the instructions of the Father; and he could say, *"I do always those things that please him."*[53]

We should demonstrate the behavior of Jesus as illustrated in the use of the Greek word *prautēs*.

The word *prautēs* is used three times of Jesus and Paul in the New Testament:

Matt 11:29: *Take My yoke upon you and learn from Me, for I am gentle* (prautēs *)and lowly in heart, and you will find rest for your souls.*

Matt 21:5: *"Tell the daughter of Zion,*
Behold, your King is coming to you,
*Lowly (*prautēs*), and sitting on a donkey,*
A colt, the foal of a donkey.' "

2 Cor. 10:1: *Now I, Paul, myself am pleading with you by the meekness* (prautēs*) and gentleness of Christ— who in presence am lowly among you, but being absent am bold toward you.*

Kenny Boles (1993) in his commentary on Galatians and Ephesians states:

> The use of *prautēs* in Scripture follows this pattern of strength brought under control. Only two individuals are described by this word in Scripture: Moses in the O.T. (Num 12:3) and Jesus three times in the N.T.... Both display the obedient response to the reins of a good horse, the gentle strength of an elephant, the ferocious courage of a watchdog to guard his master's property. Their "meekness" was not weakness; it was a heart surrendered to God, a teachable spirit, a gentle strength.[54]

The last passage I want to address that refers to the teachability of Jesus is Heb. 5:8-9: *though He was a Son, yet He learned obedience by the things which He suffered. And having been perfected, He became the author of eternal salvation to all who obey Him,*

This passage does not refer to a lack of knowledge on the part of Jesus, but of experience. The example that first comes to mind is that of Jesus in the Garden of Gethsemane when he pleads with the Father, *"If it is Your will, take this cup away from Me; nevertheless not My will, but Yours, be done."* (Luke 22:42)

Most of us can point to times when we understand something intellectually, but it takes experience to understand the depth and fullness of a concept. There are things for which education alone are insufficient. There must also be experience.

Perhaps you've heard the story of the seminar speaker who said, "When I was young, I had no children but had five theories on childrearing. Now I have five children and no theories!"

We can read all the books in the world about parenting, but until we actually become a parent we do not understand parenting. A single man or woman can teach great (and true) lessons on marriage. But until he or she has been married, there is still a lack in understanding.

So what is my point in this section? To teach that Jesus is anything less than morally perfect? No. To raise questions about the knowledge and sufficiency of Christ? Absolutely not.

My purpose, however, is to stress (to those of us who are hesitant to admit a need to be teachable) that it was a characteristic of our Lord. There are many positive examples in Scripture of teachable people. And if we desire to be like Jesus, then an attitude of teachability must be included.

The danger exists in learning by example that the lesson of the example is often too easy to miss (we just get caught up in the story) or we think it doesn't apply to our lives. But still, the easiest way to learn lessons (next to God simply laying it out and saying "Do this and don't do this") is by studying the lives of those who have preceded us: biblical examples, historical examples, and the example of the people around us in our own lives.

But we don't just learn from the example of people in history or the Bible. It is important that we learn from people in our circle of influence as well. Do people have to be dead for 100, 500, 1000, 2000 years for us to be able to learn from their example? Of course not. The advantage of learning from the examples in the Bible is that the lessons that have proven to be useful are distilled down to a few verses, a chapter or a few chapters. It is easier to distill out the lessons.

But we all need people in our lives who serve as examples. There are numerous ways to lay out whom these people are or might be.

I like Bobby Clinton's "Mentor Constellation." It can be laid out like this:

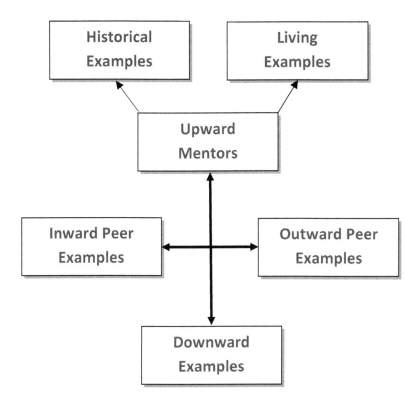

By **Historical Examples,** Clinton means those people who we will never physically meet because they are deceased, but whose life story and/or writings have been sufficiently preserved that we can come to know something about them.

It is more than just "I read a biography on that person's life or a book they wrote and I think their life or beliefs are cool." It is fine to pick up a lesson or two, but that is not what I am talking about.

It is... "Who are those people in history who have characteristics that I want to develop in my life from whom I can learn?" "Who are the people throughout history who have had a profound influence either on our world or on your field of expertise?" Where can you read to learn more about their lives, their decisions, their beliefs and actions?

You read multiple biographies of them. You read multiple writings by them. You think through their lives and decisions and how you might have reacted in similar circumstances (if you know!)

Two of my historical examples for a long time have been the early American Christian reformer and debater, Alexander Campbell, and the frontier evangelist and abolitionist Pardee Butler. Throughout the years I have read multiple books about them and have sought out articles and books that they have written. An historical example doesn't have to be an example in all ways. Alexander Campbell is an example to me in his theology and intellectual prowess. He is not an example to me in his preaching—I would never want to adapt his preaching style from the mid 19th century. Pardee Butler is an example as a church planter, an evangelist and one who was passionate about the intersection of faith and social policy. But Butler had a strong streak of anti-German racism in him (he lived during a period of a huge influx of people from Germany into the Midwest). A more recent non-Christian historical mentor for me has been Thomas Leonard: one of the founders of the modern coaching movement. He died in 2003, several years before I had heard about him. Fewer books are written about him, but I can read what resources are available, read things that he has written and listen to audios of his presentations.

By **Upward Examples**, I mean those people who are still living and who are farther down the road of life, of experience, of success who can serve as examples for you in a similar way. They can give direction and perspective. The benefit of Historical Examples is that you know how their life proceeded and ended. It is complete.

Nothing much is going to change. With Upward Examples you get to observe (from up close or from a distance) how they make decisions (at least to some degree) and how they live their lives. Their lives are not yet done: you get to see a life as it is being formed and lived. The reality is that some Upward Examples will not end well. They will make decisions or take actions that are destructive to themselves, their families or the organizations they have built. (But you can learn from even that!)

With Upward Examples you may or may not be able to actually meet them, hear them, interact with them, ask them questions.

There are Near Upward Examples and Distant Upward Examples:

Near Upward Examples are those living people who you have a personal or professional relationship or contact with from whom you can learn. Three examples of men who have served that role in my life are Dale McCann, Milt Pippenger and Ray Stinemetz. Dale was the pastor at my home church in Colorado for over 25 years. I have learned lessons about preaching, leadership, interpersonal interaction and hard work from him. Milt is a former school superintendent who also served as an elder in one of the churches I served. Milt shared a wealth of organizational experience with me. Ray was also an elder in a former church who owned an irrigation company in western Kansas. Ray (while no longer living) was during his life (and continues to be) an example to me of godliness, compassion and integrity.

The Distant Upward Examples are those people who are still living and you may be able to hear or see, but with whom you will probably never have a relationship. John Maxwell has served in this capacity for me for many years. I learned a great deal about leadership (some of it wrong) from John Maxwell. I have read scores of Maxwell's many books, have listened to hundreds of audio tapes by him and have heard Maxwell speak in huge venues, but never seen him up close, not to mention be able to ask him personal questions.

But that doesn't mean that I haven't/can't learn from him.

The third category of examples are **Peer Examples**. These are those who are walking the journey alongside you. We have much in common with them. We are in similar life or career situations. We can learn from them…and often they can learn from us. Just as there are two types of Upward Examples, there are two types of Peer Examples: Inward and Outward.

Inward Peer Examples are those who are a part of your organization: they live with many of the same relationships, policies, financial limitations that you do. They are most closely familiar with the place in life where you are.

Outward Peer Examples are those who are outside of your organization. They are in a similar life situation as you are, but may have different perspectives because of the organization that they serve or the region in which they live.

As I have developed my coaching business over the past five years, I have appreciated the lessons that I have been able to learn both from listening to the experiences as well as watching the lives and careers of other coaches.

I took a piece of paper and within 15 minutes had come up with this incomplete list:

- Carl C. and Dave B-basic coaching techniques
- Valerie C.-creativity and hustle
- Christian M.-client recruiting
- Steven F.-publicity through public speaking
- Tess D.-product development
- Mary K.-online learning
- Carol L.-social media
- Sydney R.-coaching through the stages of life

- Joseph M.-business practices and forms

- Dave J.-basics of working with small churches

- Val H.-applying coaching in a lay ministry situation.

Some of these persons would even be considered my "competitors" in certain ways, but each has been generous in sharing their knowledge and expertise.

If I am being honest there are also some that come to mind through which I have learned lots of things NOT to do. (I won't give shout-outs to them here, however!)

The fourth category of examples are the **downward examples**. The reason that I include this is because just as we have received, we are expected to give. Who are those who are a few steps behind us on the road of life with whom we can share insights, lessons and help? The beauty of this is that in being an example for others, I always gain much in inspiration and insight from those that I am mentoring. This is a hopefully a goal towards which all parents strive: to be a downward example to their children. This is (frankly) a main reason why I chose to go into coaching: from early on, God has put people into my life for whom I can build a relationship, be an example, share insights…and learn from.

I think that there can be a misunderstanding about downward examples, however. It is easy for us to misunderstand the concept and think that we become someone's guru. They watch us and model everything they do after what we do. That is not only impossible to do, it is also unhealthy.

We can be downward examples to those around us in a multitude of ways. That doesn't mean that we can project one image in one area of what we want people to see and live a contrary lifestyle in other areas. It is just that not every person needs to model themselves after us in every area of our lives. I mentor coaches who are striving to become qualified to attain their coaching accreditation with the International Coach Federation. I can be a downward example to them in that area of my life and can help them build themselves up so that they will pass the oral exam for that accreditation. In other areas of my life, it is mostly irrelevant for me to be a downward example for them. I co-lead a men's discipleship group with another man. Part of our role is being a transparent downward example for the other men in the specific areas in which we are discipling them. In other areas, some of them could be mentors to me!

We all need examples in our lives: upward examples, historical examples, peer examples (inward and outward peer example) and we need to be downward examples to others.

God teaches us

1.   Through precepts and principles

2.   Through the example of others.

We will look at the third grouping of ways that God teaches us in the next chapter.

I'll close this chapter with two quotes from that famous theologian, musician, philosopher, physician, and medical missionary in Africa Albert Schweitzer:

"Example is leadership."

"Example is not the main thing in influencing others. It is the only thing."

Chapter 6: Questions for Personal Thought and Group Discussion

- Who is a Bible character that you could learn from? Use the chart on p. 90 to analyze that person's life. What do you learn? How might this change your behavior?

- How have you seen Walt Hendrichsen's truth illustrated that Satan uses the same methods from generation to generation, because they overwhelmingly work?

- How does it affect you to think about the fact that Jesus was teachable? How does this motivate you?

- Who has God placed around you that you can learn from by their example?

  o Historical Examples?

  o Upward Examples?

  o Peer Examples?
    ✓ Outward

    ✓ Inward

  o Downward Examples?

Fable #7: The Mouse Who Thought He Was Too Small

The small mouse knew he could run fast. He loved little more than sitting on the rocks, watching the eagles make lazy circles up in the sky.

"You must be careful", said father mouse. "Eagles love to eat tender mice."

"Oh, I am so small. He wouldn't want to eat me."

"Beware, beware," said the father mouse.

"But I am quick. If I could see the eagle coming, I could dart away."

"Beware, beware," said the father mouse.

The next day the small mouse and his best friend were sitting on top of the rocks watching the eagles make lazy circles up in the sky.

The small mouse said to his friend, "My father says we are in danger here. But the eagles are so high and so far away. We are not in danger."

Suddenly, unseen by either mouse a smaller eagle swept in from behind them and grabbed the small mouse's friend and headed towards the eagle's lair.

The little mouse, knowing that he would never see his friend again, cried as he ran away. "My friend, my friend. I have learned my lesson. I will never sit on the rocks again and watch the eagles make lazy circles up in the sky."

Moral: Sometimes terrible grief is what it takes for us to learn a lesson.

CHAPTER 7: THE HARDEST WAY TO LEARN— TRAGEDY OR LARGE FAILURES.
How Does God Teach? Pt. 3

Defeat may serve as well as victory to shake the soul and let the glory out."
--Sen. Sam Ervin, Jr.

Good people are good because they've come to wisdom through failure. We get very little wisdom from success, you know."
--William Sarayan

I truly wish that being teachable was all butterflies and daffodils: easy and light. We simply study the Bible's precepts and principles and look at the example of others and we will live happily ever after. Right? Of course, that is not true. We are a part of fallen humanity. Because of that fallenness, even as regenerated believers, there is part of us that resists learning the lessons that we are needing to learn.

But God loves us enough not to let us go. He knows that sometimes (often?) we have to "learn things the hard way."

On the one hand, personal tragedies and large failures are extremely painful and often have life-long negative consequences. On the other hand, most of us learn those lessons better and remember them for years and years to come, if not forever. There are lessons we must learn that only failure can teach. That is not prescriptive (the way it SHOULD be), but descriptive (the way humans, unfortunately, are).

That is why I began this section of chapters on "How God Teaches" with the story of Daniel in the coffee shop, fearful of going home.

- The financial irresponsibility

- The pornography

- The verbal cynicism

- The religious façade

- The refusal to go for help with a counselor

The words from the preacher and from Ephesians 5 on Sunday had not reached past the hard veneer of his thoughts to actually pierce his heart. The example of others would not/ perhaps could not touch Daniel's heart.

It was going to take Daniel's world falling apart: Brenda moving out, to shake him to the point where perhaps he could be teachable. Will he? I hope so. Or will he simply see this as another example of her "unreasonableness" and allow the marriage to permanently crumble. I don't know. Hard times in life do not guarantee that any of us will learn lessons. It simply gives us another…much louder…reminder of the lesson that needs to be learned. An opportunity.

But it is certain that this opportunity to learn the lessons he needs will be very painful for Daniel.

Brian Houston, from Hillsong Church said in that excellent series on "A Teachable Spirit" that I referred to above: "Teachability is never tested on the easy things. It is only tested on the things dealing with your soul; the things that wire us inside."[55]

What are some of the harder ways of learning through which God teaches us? As has been the case in much of this book, the specific ways are too numerous to list, but let me highlight just a few prominent ones:

Failure

Most of us run so strongly from failure that we miss the learning that is in it. Part of my inability to respond to my wife's question

"So, what have you learned" that summer day was that I was still paralyzed by failure.

I was still in the grip of thinking that since I had failed, then I was a failure.[56] That was not at all the case. It was an assignment failure: in nine years of investing in one specific congregation we had been unable to turn the growth and unity around in a positive way. The church already divided and in decline before I ever showed up. But that did not mean that I personally was a failure or that I had failed in this career. Neither were true.

John Maxwell also notes "One of the greatest problems people have with failure is that they are too quick to judge isolated situations in their lives and label them as failures. Instead, they need to keep the bigger picture in mind."[57]

Proverbs says that a wise person is willing to see and heed the lessons in failure. (Proverbs 17:10: *A rebuke impresses a discerning person more than a hundred lashes a fool*.) I see failure as more of a type of rebuke than a judgment of worth.

The Example of Peter

When we think of Peter, at times we may think his only failure was when he denied Jesus three times at His arrest. (And that was certainly a failure.) But there is another, perhaps even more surprising story of failure in the life of Peter. It is a story that we might not want to accept as true unless it came from the hand of the apostle Paul.

The apostle Peter had been the one who had opened the doors of the kingdom of God to both Jews (Acts 2) as well as non-Jews (Samaritans – Acts 8:14-17; and then Gentiles – Acts 10). While it took some convincing by the Lord and a miraculous vision, Peter eventually responded to the invitation of a Roman officer named Cornelius.

Whether Peter was familiar with Cornelius from the past or Cornelius told Peter of their familiarity with the life and death of Jesus and of the nascent Christian movement, we are not told. But Peter acknowledged their knowledge and interest.

As Peter spoke to Cornelius and his household, Luke records:

"… the Holy Spirit came on all who heard the message. The circumcised believers who had come with Peter were astonished that the gift of the Holy Spirit had been poured out even on Gentiles. For they heard them speaking in tongues and praising God."

At that, the sign that God accepted the faith of non-Jews alike as saving faith, exactly as he had accepted the faith of Jews, he called for the baptism of this Gentile family into the body of Christ.

Later, in Acts 15, when a debate arose about the propriety of allowing uncircumcised Gentiles to accept the Gospel message, the very first church council was called. Christian leaders were called together to deal with this rising crisis.

After hearing the accusations of those who would exclude Gentiles, Peter arose and addressed the council:

"Brothers, you know that some time ago God made a choice among you that the Gentiles might hear from my lips the message of the gospel and believe. God, who knows the heart, showed that he accepted them by giving the Holy Spirit to them, just as he did to us. He did not discriminate between us and them, for he purified their hearts by faith. Now then, why do you try to test God by putting on the necks of Gentiles a yoke that neither we nor our ancestors have been able to bear? No! We believe it is through the grace of our Lord Jesus that we are saved, just as they are." (Acts 15:7-11).

The end of the matter was that Gentiles were allowed to come into the church without first having to undergo the Jewish initiation of circumcision or abide by the Jewish purity laws.

So, considering the pivotal part that Peter played in opening the door of the Gospel to Gentiles, his behavior in Antioch, recorded in Gal. 2:11-14 seems incomprehensible:

> *When Cephas came to Antioch, I [the apostle Paul] opposed him to his face, because he stood condemned. For before certain people came from James, he used to eat with the Gentiles. But when they arrived, he began to draw back and separate himself from the Gentiles because he was afraid of those who belonged to the circumcision group. The other Jews joined him in his hypocrisy, so that by their hypocrisy even Barnabas was led astray.*

> *When I saw that they were not acting in line with the truth of the gospel, I said to Cephas in front of them all, "You are a Jew, yet you live like a Gentile and not like a Jew. How is it, then, that you force Gentiles to follow Jewish customs?"*

I wonder if Paul thought in his mind the same thing that President Ronald Reagan used in debates first with Jimmy Carter (1980) and then Walter Mondale (1984): "There you go again…!"

Peter was wrong. He reacted, not out of conviction or truth, but out of fear, specifically fear of leaders who came from Jerusalem and either were sent by James, or at least were in his circle of associates and friends. He had led others (including his close friend Barnabas) into sin. He had been a poor witness as a leader of the church, so much that another leader had to rebuke him.

It is not clear where the account of Paul's rebuke of Peter ends (either v. 14 or v. 21 or somewhere in between) and his teaching to the Galatians picks back up, but he stresses both that salvation does not come from keeping the Jewish laws and that even if the Gentiles had not been "clean enough" (he does not relinquish that point), it is STILL not inappropriate to fellowship with them: *"But if, in seeking to be justified in Christ, we Jews find ourselves also among the sinners, doesn't that mean that Christ promotes sin? Absolutely not!"* (Gal 2.17)

If teachableness involves not simply cognitive knowledge and agreement, but also action, then Peter had a need to be teachable.

Did Peter need to be taught to BELIEVE differently, or taught to ACT differently?

While it is certain that Peter needed to be taught to ACT differently, it IS also possible that Peter needed to be taught to believe differently.

1. His belief was governed by fear of others and what they might think.

2. Believing that the value of the opinion of Jewish-Christian leaders was greater than the value of the Gentile believers around him.

It is to his credit that while we are not told what Peter's reaction was, we have no indication that he was anything but gracious in responding to the rebuke of Paul.

I appreciate a list of eight questions coined by John Maxwell to use in addressing times of failure, seeking to milk them of every bit of wisdom and benefit:

*   What caused the failure; the situation, someone else, or self?

*   Was what happened truly a failure, or did I just fall short?

*   What successes are contained in the failure?

*   What can I learn from what happened?

*   Am I grateful for the experience?

*   How can I turn this into a success?

*   Who can help me with this issue?

*   Where do I go from here?[58]

Discipline/Chastisement

A second major way in which God teaches us that is difficult to experience is through discipline and chastisement.

The Baker Encyclopedia of the Bible defines "discipline as:

Learning that molds character and enforces correct behavior; from a Latin word meaning "instruction" or "training." To discipline a person or a group means to put them in a state of good order so that they function in the way intended. Discipline, in spite of a popular misconception, is not inherently stern or harsh.[59]

The word "discipline" only appears one time in the King James translation of the Bible, but there are a host of synonyms for it, both negative ("reproof," "warning," "restraint," "correction," or "chastisement") and positive ("upbringing," "training," "instruction," and "education").

Two prominent Bible examples come to mind: David and the sexually immoral young man in Corinth.

David had sinned greatly: he not only had committed adultery with his neighbor's wife Bathsheba, but once he discovered Bathsheba was pregnant, he plotted to have her husband Uriah killed.

God's discipline came in two forms: the rebuke of Nathan and the death of the infant child.

Nathan's rebuke was a master example of coaching. He did not come out directly and accuse David of his sin. Instead he created a metaphor: a story of a poor man who had nothing but a little ewe lamb; and a rich man, who had many sheep and cattle. When the rich man had visitors and wanted to prepare a meal for them, instead of taking from his own flocks and herds, he took the lamb of the poor man, killed, cooked and served it.

When David's wrath had been sufficiently fired against someone who would do such an evil thing, Nathan dropped the bomb:

Then Nathan said to David,

You are the man! This is what the LORD, the God of Israel, says: 'I anointed you king over Israel, and I delivered you from the hand of Saul. I gave your master's house to you, and your master's wives into your arms. I gave you all Israel and Judah. And if all this had been too little, I would have given you even more. Why did you despise the word of the LORD by doing what is evil in his eyes? You struck down Uriah the Hittite with the sword and took his wife to be your own. (2 Samuel 12:7-9)

Failure on the part of David led to profound repentance and a new way of living. The apostle Paul in Acts 13:22 confirms that approbation that Samuel gave of David even before his inauguration as king (I Samuel 13:14): David was *"a man after [God's] own heart"*.

In the story of the sexually immoral young man in Corinth, Paul is writing both to correct the church there as well as to correct the young man, through them. It appears that the young man—a part of the Corinth church fellowship-- was sleeping with his step-mother. The church at Corinth not only knew about the sin, but bragged about how broad-minded and grace-filled they were!

Paul wrote to the church in Corinth, and in his letter he takes a strong stand that the church should put the young man out of the church.

Shouldn't you rather have gone into mourning and have put out of your fellowship the man who has been doing this? …So when you are assembled … and the power of our Lord Jesus is present, hand this man over to Satan for the destruction of the flesh, so that his spirit may be saved on the day of the Lord. (I Cor 5:2, 4-5)

It must be remembered that this action was not primarily a punitive one. It was intended to be redemptive. Paul says to *"hand this man over to Satan for the destruction of the flesh, so that his spirit may be saved on the day of the Lord."* That redemptive aspect is affirmed in 2 Corinthians. Apparently the young man repented of his sin and changed his behavior. Now Paul had to encourage the church to restore him—the purpose was not simply punishment—it was that he may be redeemed:

The punishment inflicted on him by the majority is sufficient. Now instead, you ought to forgive and comfort him, so that he will not be overwhelmed by excessive sorrow. I urge you, therefore, to reaffirm your love for him. (2 Cor. 2:6-8)

God's discipline is redemptive. He desires us to learn and to grow more into the image of his Son. It is evidence of God's love. But it is also painful. Just ask David if it was painful to have to watch his child die and then be rebuked by the most powerful prophet in the country. Of course it was painful. Just ask the young man in Corinth whether being cast out of the church and handed *"over to Satan for the destruction of the flesh"* was painful. Of course it was. But God's ultimate purpose in both cases was redemptive—he wanted them to learn and follow God more closely.

I think it is important when talking about chastisement to clarify what chastisement is not: it is not the same as condemnation or shaming.

The whole purpose of God's chastisement—including harsh punishment is redemptive. God's purpose is founded on the conviction that each of us has worth and value and we can do better, we can reach higher, we can live more consistently. That is what we must communicate in any chastisement in which we give to others.

Condemnation implies that there is no hope for improvement. Existential shame relates to a lack of value and worth of a person. (I will say more below about the difference between behavioral shame and existential shame later).

While it may be a debatable point, I would assert that it is never our place to condemn or shame. One of my core life philosophies is "While there is life in the body, there is hope for the soul."

Traumatic Events

The third category of harder ways of learning through which

God teaches us is "Traumatic Events."

I'm not even going to get into the topic of whether or not God brings traumatic events into our lives: that is an entirely different subject.

My emphasis is: No matter WHY or HOW they come, God uses traumatic events to teach us.

My conviction is this:

- God knows the lessons I need to learn.

- God knows the timing in which I need to learn them.

- God knows the response I will give (even if it is that I won't learn the lesson).

One of my favorite examples of this is the jailer who imprisoned the apostle Paul when he was in Philippi.

The story is in Acts 16. Paul has entered Europe for the first time (from Asia Minor) to preach the good news of Christ. There in the Greek city of Philippi they were going to a local place of prayer where they were approached by a female slave who was a fortune-teller. (She did so, Luke says, by the power of a demon within her). Seeing Paul and Silas, she began to cry out, *"These men are servants of the Most High God, who are telling you the way to be saved."* (Acts 16:17b)

Perhaps Paul did not want their message to be delivered this way, perhaps he felt it undercut the authority of their message to have it declared by a known demon-possessed girl. Luke says that Paul was weary of the girl shouting it wherever they were. (She kept this up for many days.) Finally Paul became so annoyed that he turned around and said to the spirit, *"In the name of Jesus Christ I command you to come out of her!" At that moment the spirit left her."* (Acts 16:18)

The owners of the slave girl were so upset that their ticket to financial prosperity had been denied them that they grabbed Paul and Silas and took them before the city magistrates, making false accusations. The crowd attacked Paul and Silas and the magistrates had them stripped and flogged with rods. They were then thrown into prison.

The jailer was commanded to keep them securely imprisoned, and so he *"locked them in the inner cell and fastened their feet in stocks."* (16:24b) There is no indication that he was favorably disposed to Paul and Silas at all.

Then, the story goes, about midnight *"there was such a violent earthquake that the foundations of the prison were shaken. At once all the prison doors flew open, and everyone's chains came loose. The jailer woke up, and when he saw the prison doors open, he drew his sword and was about to kill himself because he thought the prisoners had escaped."* (16:26b-27)

Terrible tragedy had struck this man. The responsibility for keeping all of the prisoners, especially Paul and Silas had been committed to him. The earthquake had (he presumed) allowed all of the prisoners to escape. The penalty from Rome for such a failure of responsibility (even in the face of natural events like an earthquake, apparently) would be the death sentence for the jailer. Rather than face that, he was ready to take his own life.

Paul and Barnabas stepped in and assured them that they and all of the other prisoners were still there: none had escaped, even though they had the chance. The response of the jailer was *"Sirs, what must I do to be saved?"* (v. 30). The jailer's life had been physically saved. Those who say that the jailer was asking a purely secular question ("What can I do to keep from being killed by the government officials because of this prison break?") miss the point. Perhaps he had heard the testimony of the slave girl. Perhaps he had heard parts of Paul's preaching over the past several days. Perhaps he went to sleep hearing the hymns that Paul and Silas were singing in their imprisonment. Whatever had transpired, we don't know. What we do know is that his heart was ready. Daniel Polhill states, "The miracle of the earthquake and the prisoners who wouldn't flee arrested his attention and prepared his heart to receive Paul's message."[60]

Paul and Silas declared: *"Believe in the Lord Jesus, and you will be saved—you and your household."* They then preached the message of the Gospel of Christ to them and the jailer and his family became believers that very night. The jailer washed Paul and Silas' wounds and even took them to his own private house for a meal.

The next day the magistrates came and released Paul and Silas and the two went (along with the jailer and his family we presume) and met with the rest of the Christian believers in the city. The next day Paul and Silas left Philippi and we never hear of the jailer again.

What can be seen from this story?

First, God had a lesson that he wanted the jailer to learn and he wanted the jailer and his family to come to faith in him. If the owners of the slave girl had not reacted in anger to Paul's actions and drug them before the magistrates, the jailer would never have met them. If the magistrates had released the men without jailing them, the crisis that led to his conversion would not have taken place!

Second, God knew the timing that was needed to bring this jailer to such a mindset that he would be receptive to the Gospel. Whether God caused the earthquake or was knowledgeable about when it would occur and worked so that all of the players were in the right place at the right time seem equally miraculous to me.

Third, God knew the response of the jailer. He knew exactly the right circumstances that needed to happen at just the right time in order for the jailer to have the opportunity to learn the lesson God wanted him to learn.

In speaking of learning from events in the Bible, it is important not to minimize the trauma of those events, even though we recognize the learning within them. At times our emotional attachment to the stories of the Bible causes a patina to begin to cover the accounts such that we see the learning and the end results and the beauty of how God works without recognizing the trauma that was involved for those who endured the actual events.

Sam James did not know what he would find, if anything of his former work in Vietnam. He had served as a missionary and seminary teacher there during the last years of South Vietnam. But when he had fled by night as North Vietnamese tanks rolled into Saigon, the seminary was closed and the churches were about to be closed. He knew that most of those Vietnamese Christians with whom he had worked had suffered years of prison, "re-education" camps and persecution for following Christ.

Fifteen years later, he planned to return. He sent word to Vietnamese Christian friends that he was coming, but realistically did not believe he would be able to reunite with any of them.

One day during his visit someone brushed up against him on the street and handed him a handwritten note: "Meet us at the park at 2 o'clock." Not knowing what he would find, he arrived at 2:00. A single man led him through a field of high tangled weeds to a small clearing. In that clearing, sitting around an old wrought iron table were seven of his former seminary students.

At first Sam had trouble recognizing them because they were so frail and gaunt. They greeted him with tears and laughter and spoke of the persecution they had endured under communism.

As they spoke, one thing struck James: when these seven men had arrived at the seminary they were from the country and were rough and unruly. He was more accustomed to the learned and sophisticated students that came from the cities. He doubted if these rural men would even make it through one of the seminary classes, not to mention finish the degree or even more…endure years of harsh persecution.

And yet these were the ones who had endured. They had

persevered and led the persecuted church during terrible days. Sam James later said, "It just shows how God's transforming power can take anybody --*anybody* -- and make us into what he wants us to be."

In the middle of their time together one of the men pulled out an aluminum tray and set it on the rusty wrought iron table. Another man pulled out a loaf of bread and still another a small bunch of grapes. These were set on the tray. One of the men broke the bread and passed it around and then each man took a single grape. "Nobody said it was the Lord's Supper, but we knew what it was."[61]

Extreme trauma had taught each of these men how to become leaders and more faithful disciples of Jesus Christ. It sounds glib for an outsider to say it but it is true: God knew the lessons they needed to learn; He knew the timing in which they needed to learn it and He knew the response that each one would give.

Grief

Elizabeth Kübler-Ross did the world a great service in her work on dying and grief. While not all agree on the stages that both dying and grieving persons go through, it is generally recognized that there are "tasks" that grieving people go through. They are basically the same "tasks" that dying people go through:

Denial-a conscious or unconscious effort to deny the facts as they exist.

Anger-anger can be focused in different directions and sometimes all at the same time: anger at self, anger at those around the grieving person, anger at the one who has died, anger at God, anger at other authority figures.

Bargaining-in the normal dying process, it is common for the dying person to bargain with God (or whomever they see God to be): "If you spare my life, I'll never smoke again, drink again, swear again." Grieving people can be incredibly irrational in their grief, making promises to God if only He will bring back their loved one from the dead. In relational grief (such as a relational break-up) the bargaining may take the form of "But can't we still be friends?"

Depression-the beginning seeds of acceptance have begun- to be internalized, but the loss is so great that the person feels they cannot cope. They have begun to accept what has happened but it is so great that there is not only great sadness, fear, and regret, but often there is an emotional numbness.

Acceptance-this stage does NOT mean that we are OK with what happened. But we are beginning to be able to emotionally detach from it and begin to see the situation more objectively without the cloudiness of emotion.

Why do I bring these well-known stages of dying and grief to your attention? Because too many well-meaning friends and family, in the desire to help the grieving one "learn the lessons of the situation" make grievous and hurtful mistakes. The friends and family may see a lesson in the situation, but that does not mean that it is the same lesson that will be drawn by the grieving one, or that they are ready to come to the point where they objectively can see what they can learn from the situation.

I speak from experience. I was unable to give an answer to my wife, "So, what have you learned in the past six months" partly because the learning journey was not anywhere near done, but also because I was still in the process of grieving. Grieving a ministry ended, relationships ended…some by betrayal, the loss of income, perhaps the permanent loss of a pastoral ministry career. And that does not begin to take into account my grief over my cancer diagnosis, surgery and after-effects. I was still in high grief mode when she asked the question. Whether or not I SHOULD have been in high grief mode at that point is really irrelevant: a person is where they are in their grief journey irrespective of anyone else's opinion of where they "should" be.

There are many other types of incredibly painful experiences besides failure, discipline and traumatic experiences through which God teaches us, but I have highlighted just these few.

As we go through times of failure, discipline of trauma, there are two reactions of which we need to be cautious:

Hardness of Heart

In speaking of God's discipline of his children, the writer of Hebrews quotes from the writer of Proverbs in 12:5-6,

And have you completely forgotten this word of encouragement that addresses you as a father addresses his son? It says, "My son, do not make light of the Lord's discipline, and do not lose heart when he rebukes you, because the Lord disciplines the one he loves, and he chastens everyone he accepts as his son.[62]

The Bible speaks metaphorically of a "hard heart." When it does so, the Bible refers to "the act of an evil person's strengthening of resolve to counter an action that God desires."[63]

I have spoken extensively about hardheartedness back in chapter 4, so I won't just duplicate that here. The point is that we are often tempted to let failure lead us to hardheartedness. But we dare not.

False Shame (Behavioral Shame versus Existential Shame)

A common reaction to tragedy or failure is to feel overwhelmed by shame.

Defining shame and guilt can be as tricky as defining teachableness. An article in *Psychology Today* lays out the difference in these words:

Guilt and shame sometimes go hand in hand; the same action may give rise to feelings of both shame and guilt, where the former reflects how we feel about ourselves and the latter involves an awareness that our actions have injured someone else. In other words, shame relates to self, guilt to others.[64]

On the other hand, in the world of addiction recovery, a different distinction is often made between guilt and shame. Guilt, it is said, is negative emotion based on what we have done, while shame is negative emotion based on who we are.

This second definition feels right, but it doesn't jive with how the Bible uses the term.

The Bible speaks of shame in affirming terms: there are times that shame is appropriate. Shame is the negative emotion we feel when we have sinned against God. (Jer. 2:26: *"As a thief is shamed when caught, so the house of Israel shall be shamed— they, their kings, their officials, their priests, and their prophets"*). Shame is performance based, i.e. it is an appropriate emotion in response to having done something wrong or failed to do something right. (Prov. 14.34: *Doing what is right lifts people up. But sin brings shame to any nation.* (NIrV)

I like how the *HarperCollins Bible Dictionary* puts it:

"The biblical writers believed that there should be a natural sense of disgrace and unworthiness when one offended God or one's companions. It was considered appalling when people no longer had any sense of shame." (cf. Jer. 6:15; also Job 19:3)."[65]

But just as there is true guilt and false guilt, so there is true shame and false shame. False shame deals more in the existential realm of shame for who one is rather than what one has done.

The writer of Hebrews speaks of Jesus' rejection of shame on the cross: *"For the joy set before him he [Jesus] endured the cross, scorning its shame, and sat down at the right hand of the throne of God."* (Hebrews 12:2)

There are times to reject shame. It comes down to being able to separate what I have done from who I am. I can feel guilt and shame for what I have done. But it is a different matter to feel shame for who one is. To feel shame for who one is as a child of God who is forgiven of sin is inappropriate. It is a denial of the efficacy of the work of Christ on the cross.

Failures (especially large failures) can paralyze us. They can strike at the core of who we are (or who we see ourselves to be). The message of the cross, however, is that while there are times where it is appropriate to feel shame for what we have done (particularly in the realm of moral failures), in Christ it is never appropriate to feel shame for who we are.

Some Suggestions

The Christian life is a life of discipleship. The very word "disciple" ("follower") implies the idea of banding together with other disciples. Here are some suggestions for being teachable in the difficult times of life:

1. You probably don't see your own unteachableness. Ask someone whom you trust, but who will also be frank with you.

2. Find a coach or mentor and be totally honest.

3. Begin a listening habit—realize that you fight with God when you don't listen.

4. Learn godly character.

5. Change what you read and look at.

Conclusion

So what do we make of the lessons that come our way through means of failure or personal tragedy?

- God knows the lessons I need to learn.

- God knows the timing in which I need to learn them.

- God knows the response I will give (even if it is that I won't learn the lesson).

May my response be to cooperate with him instead of responding with a hard heart and rebellion.

Chapter 7: Questions for Personal Thought and Group Discussion

- Are you a person who has to "learn things the hard way?" If so, why do you think that is?

- What was your reaction to the Brian Houston quote: "Teachability is never tested on the easy things. It is only tested on the things dealing with your soul; the things that wire us inside"?

- What lessons has God taught you through:
  - Failure?

  - Discipline/Chastisement?

  - Traumatic Events?

  - Grief?

  - Hardness of Heart?

  - False Shame?

- When was an instance in which asking John Maxwell's eight questions for times of failure would have helped you learn the lessons of failure in the past? How can you remember them for the future?

- How can you implement the five steps for being teachable in the difficult times of life:

    o Ask someone whom you trust, but who will also be frank with you about the areas in your life in which you may be unteachable.

    o Find a coach or mentor and be totally honest.

    o Begin a listening habit—realize that you fight with God when you don't listen.

    o Learn godly character.

    o Change what you read and look at.

Fable #8: The Baby Worm Who Would Not Learn

The baby worm made his way to the surface of the ground following the tunnel built by his mother. As they reached the top, his mother said, "Curly, I want you to begin to dig your own tunnel."

"I can't, mother," whined Curly. "I could never build as fine a tunnel as yours. I would fail and everyone would laugh."

"But you will need to know how to dig your own tunnel when danger comes," replied his mother.

"Oh, I will find a way," said the baby worm.

The mother then said "I need you to learn how to stretch yourself out and look like a twig so that the birds won't know you are a worm and come and eat you."

"But I'm NOT a twig," complained Curly. "I know I could never fool anyone by just stretching straight. I would fail at that."

"But you will need to know how to disguise yourself when danger comes," replied his mother.

"Oh, I will find a way," said the baby worm.

The worm mother then said, "My child, if you will not learn to dig or hide, you must learn how to sink your spikes down into the dirt so an enemy cannot pull you off the ground. If your spikes are strong enough, the enemy will tire and leave you before your spikes come lose."

"My spikes are small and worthless. I am just a child. If I tried that I would fail. There is no use wasting my time and failing to be able to sink my spikes down far enough into the ground."

"But you will need to know how to hold on when danger

comes," replied his mother.

"Oh, I will find a way," said the baby worm.

The mother shook her head and went off to forage for food.

Suddenly the shadow of a robin passed over the baby worm. The baby worm saw the danger as the robin landed close by. But he knew of no way to protect himself. He had not learned to dig, or to disguise himself or to sink down his spikes.

As the robin carried him away to her nest to feed to her young, the young worm cried, "Oh why was I not willing even to try?"

Moral: "If you are afraid to fail in small things you will surely fail in big things."

CHAPTER 8: TEN WAYS TO INCREASE YOUR TEACHABLENESS

"When the student is ready, the teacher will appear."
—*unknown (often wrongly credited to the Buddha)*

As a personal and executive coach, I begin every coaching relationship with the understanding that we can all grow in whatever areas we want. There is no area of our life in which we cannot work to grow and improve. But that wasn't a new message for me when I became a coach.

The New Testament is full of admonitions and encouragement to grow:

- God activates the growth of the Gospel to grow through the planting and watering of his servants (1 Co 3:6).

- Our faith is to *"continue to grow"* (2 Co 10:15).

- We are to grow into maturity in Christ (Eph 4:15).

- The spiritual body is to grow. (Col 2:19).

- We are to grow up in our salvation (1 Pe 2:2).

- We are *"grow in the grace and knowledge of our Lord and Savior Jesus Christ."* (2 Pet. 3:18).

The same is true in regard to teachableness: surely there are ways we can grow in our ability to be teachable. I began this chapter with the proverb: "When the student is ready, the teacher will appear." That proverb can either be seen mystically, or practically. If we see it mystically we would say that God (or "the universe" in non-Christian parlance) knows when we are ready to learn a lesson and when we are, the one who is to teach us will be sent to us.

If we see it more practically, it speaks to readiness. When I am ready to learn a lesson, I will be able to see those who can teach me that lesson who are already around me. They may have already been around me, but I could not recognize that because I was not yet ready to learn that lesson.

"**Readiness** implies a degree of single-mindedness and eagerness. Individuals learn best when they are physically, mentally, and emotionally ready to learn, and they do not learn well if they see no reason for learning."[66]

Howard Hendricks, Christian educator and professor at Dallas Theological Seminary for over 50 years has taken the *Seven Laws of Teaching*[67] made famous by John Milton Gregory and revised them into "The Seven Laws of the Teacher". Hendricks' seventh law is "The Law of Readiness." That law states: "The teaching-learning process will be most effective when both student and teacher are adequately prepared."[68]

Many of us are familiar with the concept of readiness when it comes to education. Helping children become ready for school has become an important cause over the past twenty-five years. We can debate the reasons why children are not deemed ready for school and whether certain actions to address that are effective or good social policy, but the reality is that too many children begin school not prepared to learn.

President George H.W. Bush and 50 state governors established the National Education Goals Project (NEGP) in 1990. The very first goal of that educational panel was "by the year 2000, all children in America will start school ready to learn."

What criteria did they use to determine that? There were five dimensions listed by the panel as integral in readiness.

- Physical Well-Being and Motor Development (What is the child's health status? Do they appear nourished, rested and are they immunized?)

- <u>Social/Emotional Development</u> (Can the child play and work cooperatively, adapt to planned activities and changes, and respond appropriately to a variety of situations?)

- <u>Approach to Learning</u> (Is the child curious about new things and situations?)

- <u>Language Development</u> (Can the child communicate what they want and need in an appropriate language?)

- <u>Cognition and General Knowledge</u> (Can the child follow simple, two-step directions?)[69]

Between Gregory and Hendricks was the psychologist Edward Thorndike, professor at Teachers College at Columbia University. He, likewise, developed theories of learning and, likewise, enunciated a Law of Readiness. He stated it a bit differently: "The law of readiness states that a learner's satisfaction is determined by the extent of his preparatory set, that is, his readiness for action. "

This law was summarized into two parts:

- When someone is ready to perform an act, to do so is satisfying.

- When someone is ready to perform some act, not to do so is annoying. An interference with goal-directed behavior causes frustration and making someone to do something he does not want to do is frustrating."

The bottom line appears to be a recognition that teachability involves being ready to learn a new lesson. We see the need for it and understand some basic elements of the item/lesson we are about to learn. Not learning it can even be irritating.

I have avoided using the term "teachable moments" so far in this book. That is because the phrase "teachable moments" is pretty much a cliché. For example if I say the phrase "teachable ___(blank)___" what pops into your mind? For most people it is "teachable moment or moments."

Clichés are those phrases that are used so commonly that we don't have to think about what they mean…everyone presumes that we know. And that is the problem…we don't have to think…and everyone DOESN'T define them the same. But clichéd or not, the concept of "teachable moments" is a valid one.

Beth Lewis defines "teachable moment" as "an unplanned opportunity that arises in the classroom where a teacher has an ideal chance to offer insight to his or her students."[70]

On the spiritual plane, teachable moments are those times when our need for God's instruction and our awareness of our need for God's instruction come together. God seems to have a wonderful way of bringing people and situations into our lives at those moments to teach us the lessons he has for us.

Here are two examples of teachable moments in the life of Jesus:

1. Matt 12:46-50-Jesus found a teachable moment when his mother and brothers came to where he was teaching. We do not know the exact location except it was in Galilee. (Of course Jesus' childhood home, Nazareth, was also in Galilee.) Jesus' relationship with his siblings, particularly seems strained because they did not understand why their brother was so different. But while he was teaching, Jesus' mother and brothers arrived and sent someone to where Jesus was to call him out to see them. When Jesus was told of their presence and desire to speak with him, he found a "teachable moment" and spoke of his true family: those who do the will of his Father in heaven. *"He replied to him, 'Who is my mother, and who are my brothers?' Pointing to his disciples, he said, "Here are my mother and my brothers. For whoever does the will of my Father in heaven is my brother and sister and mother."*

2.   Further on in Matthew's gospel he tells of Jesus' strong and stinging rebuke of Peter (Matt 16:24; compare 16:23 with 4:10). Jesus explained how it was a teachable moment for the rest of the disciples and that the cross would define not only his own future but theirs as well (cf. 10:38).

Just because it is a "teachable moment", that doesn't mean that everyone who experiences the event will learn the lesson!

Are there specific things we can do in order to be prepared to learn those lessons when life's teachable moments happens? I believe there are ten things we can do to increase our readiness, i.e. make ourselves more ready to learn:

1.   Look for the big picture

WWII General Omar Nelson Bradley is credited with saying "We need to learn to set our course by the stars, not by the lights of every passing ship."

Someone who is inexperienced in being teachable will sometimes fail to actually learn the lessons that they need to learn because they are looking at too small of a picture. They will see one lesson from an event and try to live by that. But then they will have another experience where the seeming lesson is the opposite of that. And so he or she will jump and try to behave or live a different way. Was the first lesson the one that the individual was "supposed" to learn? Perhaps; perhaps not. Was the contradictory lesson the one that the individual was "supposed" to learn? Perhaps; perhaps not.

The big picture may be: "How does this lesson fit in with the trajectory of my life/career?" "If I follow this lesson, will it hurt me more than help me, or help me more than hurt me?" "Will it hurt others? Will it help others?"

Wisdom comes in taking the long view. That is why it is

uncommon for younger adults to be truly wise. They simply haven't had enough experiences yet. They probably have learned some lessons: but some may be true and some may not be true. It is only over the long-view that we are able to see how the lessons of life fit together. Some may simply be outliers. Others may have been misinterpreted in the moment.

Failure is especially problematic when it comes to learning the correct lessons. John Maxwell says, "One of the greatest problems people have with failure is that they are too quick to judge isolated situations in their lives and label them as failures. Instead, they need to keep the bigger picture in mind."[71]

That leads to the second skill or attitude we can develop to better prepare ourselves to learn:

2.   Be willing to fail.

This is really just an extension or elaboration of #1, but we learn much less from success than we do from failures.

Failure does a couple of things for us regarding teachableness:

a.   It makes us desire to be teachable. Failure doesn't feel good. Most of us will do a great deal in order to avoid failure. And that's understandable. And in a desire to avoid failing again, many of us will look for the lessons to be learned or the attitudes to be developed that will keep us from failing again.

That is a mixed blessing in that it does put us in a learning mode, but it presumes that failing is a thing to be avoided at all cost, which it is not.

b.   The lessons of failure stick better. They are usually painful. And pain is remembered longer than pleasure. I like how one internet writer put it: "Because we tend and nurture our pains tenderly as a garden, and let our pleasures float away."[72]

We remember pain longer than pleasure because pain threatens our comfort or survival, while pleasure does not. Research has shown that (unlike pleasure) pain is not only a physical reality, but the neural pathways that carry pain signals that also excite parts of the brain dealing with emotion and cognition. "Injury messages directly excite brain structures that produce emotion, and these in turn stimulate areas of the brain that create the meaning of the immediate situation. Pain emerges into awareness only after sensory, emotional, and cognitive processes have combined to form a coherent, integrated pattern of experience."[73]

But for us to best learn…to best be teachable…we need to be willing to fail. We need to be willing to take risks, to look for ways to expose ourselves to new experiences, learning and people.[74]

One of the problems with the WAY I was let go from my job—and especially being timed with the diagnosis of having cancer—was that it enabled me to feel like a victim. The victim mentality is an escape route from responsibility. I was able to avoid facing the lessons to be learned because it was all "someone else's fault." It was only when I learned not to play the victim that I was ready to really face the lessons to be learned.

A principle that the past few years has taught me is:
> To not succeed but to learn is to grow
> To not succeed and NOT to learn is truly to fail.

I personally was challenged to ask myself about my own willingness to risk when I was introduced to "The Teachability Index".

There are several instruments called the "Teachability Index" but the one I am using measures the relationship between risk and change.

The Teachability Index looks like this:

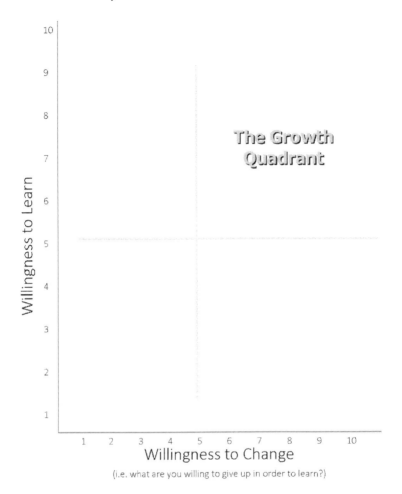

As you can see, the two axes are "Willingness to Learn" and "Willingness to Change". The vertical axis is actually the easier of the two, but both are critical. If we are going to be teachable, we must be willing to learn. Many, however, don't want to learn. We have talked about different ones in that category in this book so far.

The second axis is "Willingness to Change". Change happens on a lot of levels, but bottom line is, if you are not willing and able to change, not only will you not reach what you want, but you will fall behind…our culture is always changing. What are you willing to give up? What are you willing to do without? What are you willing to stop? Many people are willing to learn things, but they are not willing to risk anything (read: "change") to see them come to fruition. They have hopes and dreams, but they are not willing to put any money, time, reputation on the line in order to see it happen.

If your "Willingness to Learn" is a 10, but your "Willingness to Change" is a 1, your Teachability index is extremely low. The chance of you growing to where you want to be is small. If your "Willingness to Change" is a 10, but your "Willingness to Learn" is a 1, still your Teachability Index is still very low. There must be growth in both areas for us to succeed—Willingness to Learn and Willingness to Change.

But the reality in both is that we must be willing to risk failure. We must be willing to risk in order to be teachable and that includes opening ourselves up to the possibility of failure.

3. Cultivate your Listening Skills:

We cannot learn without listening. Proverbs names teachableness as a foundation to wisdom. A teachable person is one who is willing to listen.

Out in the open wisdom calls aloud, she raises her voice in the public square; on top of the wall she cries out, at the city gate she makes her speech: "How long will you who are simple love your simple ways? How long will mockers delight in mockery and fools hate knowledge? Repent at my rebuke! Then I will pour out my thoughts to you, I will make known to you my teachings. But since you refuse to listen when I call and no one pays attention when I stretch out my hand, since you disregard all my advice and do not accept my rebuke, I in turn will laugh when disaster strikes you; I will mock when calamity overtakes you—when calamity overtakes you like a storm, when disaster sweeps over you like a whirlwind, when distress and trouble overwhelm you. (Proverbs 1:20-27)

As G.K. Chesterton said, "There's a lot of difference between listening and hearing."[75]   Most people have the physical ability to hear and the mental capacity to understand the words being said (if they are in a language the person understands!).

But hearing is quite different from listening. Listening pays attention to inflection, to the emotions in and behind the words, to the context and history behind what is being said. Hearing is a physical act. Listening is an act of the will—it is something that is done with conscious intention and concentration.

To whom do we listen?

a.   Listen to God

Thomas Merton said "Just remaining quietly in the presence of God, listening to Him, being attentive to Him, requires a lot of courage and know-how."[76]

We listen to him, of course, through the Bible: the Word of God.

* 2 Timothy 3:16 : *"All Scripture is God-breathed and is useful for teaching, rebuking, correcting and training in righteousness."*

* In Heb. 3:7-11 the writer refers to the words of Psalm 95:7-11 as the words of the Holy Spirit. *("As the Holy Spirit says.")*

* 2 Peter 1:20–21: *"Above all, you must understand that no prophecy of Scripture came about by the prophet's own interpretation of things. For prophecy never had its origin in the human will, but prophets, though human, spoke from God as they were carried along by the Holy Spirit."*

But God also speaks to us through circumstances, through nature and creation, through music, through the Holy Spirit and (as we shall see below) through other people.

Andrew Murray said in *Abide in Christ*:

Among the lessons to be learnt of those who are studying the blessed art of abiding in Christ, there is none more needful and more profitable than this one of stillness of soul. In it alone can we cultivate that teachableness of spirit, to which the Lord will reveal His secrets--that meekness to which He shows His ways.[77]

Our age is not one that honors or encourages listening to God. We want to take the shortcut of having others to do the work for us. But that is dangerous.

We will be held responsible for the choices we make, not the other person. I tell my coaching clients that there are several reasons why I am a coach and not a consultant. A consultant comes in, looks at a situation and tells someone what they need to do. A coach asks questions to help the client come up with the best plan of action based on their own knowledge and values. I tell my clients, "If I tell you what to do, you will be less motivated to do it, because it comes from someone else. When the going gets tough, you will be tempted not to persevere because it is, after all, someone else's idea. There is no one, including me, who knows your situation better than you. And I won't have to live with the consequences of your actions. The worst thing that happens to me is that I lose you as a client. The negative things that can happen to you might include the loss of a sale, the loss of a job, the loss of a relationship, the loss of a family or jail! (depending on the circumstances).

It is critical that we not simply listen to others (as we will see in the next section), but it is critical that we listen to God. Since most of my coaching clients are Christians, I usually tell them of my conviction that the Holy Spirit dwells in them and is speaking to them telling them the way to go. Our job, in part, is to make them sensitive to hearing the Holy Spirit speaking to them.

Pope Paul VI reportedly said, "Of all human activities, man's listening to God is the supreme act of his reasoning and will."

b.   Listen to others

The book of Proverbs is rich with admonitions to learn from others. A brief sample:

Proverbs 12:15: *The way of fools seems right to them, but the wise listen to advice.*

Proverbs 13:13-14,20: *Whoever scorns instruction will pay for it, but whoever respects a command is rewarded. The teaching of the wise is a fountain of life, turning a person from the snares of death…. Walk with the wise and become wise, for a companion of fools suffers harm.*

Proverbs 10:8 *The wise in heart accept commands, but a chattering fool comes to ruin.*

Few of us would disagree in theory. How do we, however, overcome our natural inclination to not listen? Listen to people? Listen to God? This gets back in part between that balance we discussed earlier between intractableness and gullibility.

I would suggest nine principles to apply to any teacher, to see whether or not their teaching should be listened to:

1.   <u>Is what they say in line with what you understand of God's word to date?</u>

Paul says, *"But even if we or an angel from heaven should preach a gospel other than the one we preached to you, let them be under God's curse!"* (Gal. 1:8)

The scriptures are our plumb-line. If it is inconsistent with scripture, it must be questioned. I would further say that it is important to know not just scriptures individually, but the gist and flow of scripture altogether. A favorite tactic of many is "verse picking". The Bible can be forced to say anything anyone wants it to by picking out individual verses and using them to build a case. (My favorite example is the juxtaposition of Matthew 27:5 [*"He* [Judas] *went away and hanged himself."*] with Luke 10:47 [*"Jesus told him, 'Go and do likewise.'"*] Both are scripture. Therefore (the ludicrous example goes) to be obedient to Jesus, we need to go out and hang ourselves!)

Of course not.

Does what is taught harmonize both with the letter of scripture as well as the spirit of scripture? Is it in harmony, not just with one or two verses in the Bible but with the gist and flow of scripture?

2. <u>Do they raise the opinions and traditions of humans to the level of scripture?</u>

"He [Jesus] *replied, 'Isaiah was right when he prophesied about you hypocrites; as it is written: These people honor me with their lips, but their hearts are far from me. They worship me in vain; their teachings are merely human rules.'"* (Mark 7:6-7)

One of the saddest experiences of my years in pastoral ministry was one time when we shared our church's baptistery with a congregation of another faith tradition. They baptized by immersion as we did, but were building their new church building as the cash came in. They were in their building, but did not yet have enough money to install a baptistery tank. We were always happy to share our facilities with other churches.

But in this instance it made me very sad. I hung around the back of the church auditorium near the sound board to just witness this joyful moment in the life of that church. The preacher of the church took the baptismal candidate into the water and asked them a similar question to what I would ask of any person who presented themselves for baptism in the churches I served, "Do you believe that Jesus Christ is the Son of God and do you take him as your Lord and Savior?" The candidate answered affirmatively. The preacher then went on for a fully ten minutes (I counted them!) asking questions about the teachings of their church, some clearly taught in scripture and some clearly extrabiblical teachings. After each instance, the preacher would wait for the candidate to affirm that they did, in fact, believe this or that particular doctrine or teaching. Finally after the candidate had been properly quizzed, the preacher baptized him. This was repeated four or five times with succeeding candidates.

It is not just the Pharisees of old who put human doctrine on the same level with scripture!

3.   <u>Does the teaching further deepen your walk with the God of the Bible or weaken it?</u>

"If a prophet, or one who foretells by dreams, appears among you and announces to you a sign or wonder, and if the sign or wonder spoken of takes place, and the prophet says, "Let us follow other gods" (gods you have not known) "and let us worship them," you must not listen to the words of that prophet or dreamer. The LORD your God is testing you to find out whether you love him with all your heart and with all your soul." (Deut. 13:1-3)

4.   <u>Do they further the cause of Christian unity or create further divisions?</u>

I urge you, brothers and sisters, to watch out for those who cause divisions and put obstacles in your way that are contrary to the teaching you have learned. Keep away from them. For such people are not serving our Lord Christ, but their own appetites. By smooth talk and flattery they deceive the minds of naive people. (Romans 16:17–18)

One of my mentors was W.F. Lown, the president of the undergraduate college I attended (Manhattan Christian College). He tells the story of a conversation that had taken place early in his years as President. Someone made the comment about a preacher or elder that they both knew. The first person said that the man in question was doctrinally straight as an arrow, but was not a loving person. Dr. Lown thought for a minute and then quietly asked, "When did love stop being a doctrine?"

The type of person we are to follow should be one who furthers Christian unity and love, not someone whose main claim to fame is that they are divisive.

5.   <u>What experience does the speaker have?</u>

He must not be a recent convert, or he may become conceited and fall under the same judgment as the devil. (I Tim 3:6).

Educational attainment is definitely one qualifier, but only one of several types of experiences that could qualify a speaker. Do they have the background to know of what they speak? Do others regard their experience as a qualifying factor? Is there experience; successful experience? While failure can tell us what doesn't work (or at least didn't work in that situation) just knowing what doesn't work doesn't mean we know what does work.

6. <u>How does the speaker live? Is it consistent with his/her message?</u>

The simple believe anything, but the prudent give thought to their steps. (Prov 14:15)

Periodically the media gets hold of a Christian leader who does not live according to the lifestyle that is "expected" of a Christian leader. That may be moral issues or it may be financial issues. In the 1980s, while Jim and Tammy Faye Bakker earned a salary similar to (or less than) than that of a business executive who ran a business with the breadth of service and income levels as PTL, they were blasted (mostly fairly, I believe) for claiming to be ministers, but living the lifestyle of business moguls. People sacrificing greatly to donate to their ministry did not know that an exorbitant amount was going to the Bakker's salaries (as well as others). Their lifestyle was not consistent with their message.

7. <u>What are the practical results of their teaching?</u>

'Watch out for false prophets. They come to you in sheep's clothing, but inwardly they are ferocious wolves. By their fruit you will recognize them. Do people pick grapes from thorn bushes, or figs from thistles? Likewise, every good tree bears good fruit, but a bad tree bears bad fruit. A good tree cannot bear bad fruit, and a bad tree cannot bear good fruit. Every tree that does not bear good fruit is cut down and thrown into the fire. Thus, by their fruit you will recognize them.' (Matthew 7:15–20)

8.   What do they say about Jesus?

"This is how you can recognize the Spirit of God: Every spirit that acknowledges that Jesus Christ has come in the flesh is from God, but every spirit that does not acknowledge Jesus is not from God." (I John 4:2-3)

It has often been said (correctly) that every false religion or cult has a defective view of the person of Jesus Christ. They may have lots of things similar or different from one another, but the one thing that they all share in common is a view of Jesus that differs from the Biblical/historic understanding of who Christ is.

If I am listening to someone and things don't seem right, it is often a good idea to investigate their view of who Jesus is. Just because that is right doesn't mean that all of their teaching is right, but if that is wrong, you know things are not right and you should be cautious about listening to them.

9.   Look at who is following them: who listens to their message?

They are from the world and therefore speak from the viewpoint of the world, and the world listens to them. We are from God, and whoever knows God listens to us; but whoever is not from God does not listen to us. This is how we recognize the Spirit of truth and the spirit of falsehood. (I John 4:5-6)

We can tell a certain amount by association. (I recognize that Jesus was criticized by the Pharisees for associating with sinners, tax collectors and prostitutes, but that criticism arose out of a misunderstanding of Jesus' mission). Are those that vouch for this person, people whose judgment I respect? Do I even know who vouches for them?

So, to grow in your teachableness, you need to Look at the Big Picture, Be Willing to Fail, and third, Cultivate Your Listening Skills.

4. Develop those characteristics in your life that are the opposite of those things that hinder teachableness

In an earlier chapter we looked at those characteristics that hinder teachableness. It only makes sense that if we work to do the opposite of those things, that it should make us more teachable. The original list of things that make us unteachable were:

- Pride

- Fear

- Laziness

- Complaining and Criticism

- Sins Deceitfulness

- Callousneness/A Hard Heart

- Success and Demonstrated Talent

- An Insistence on Understanding

It seems (at least to me) to make sense to attempt to cultivate the positive traits that are the opposite of those eight negative traits.

I would group them as below. In order to develop teachableness, we need to strive to build...

a. Faith (which counters "An Insistence on Understanding")

b. Humility (which counters "Pride" and "Success and Demonstrated Talent")

c. Trust in God (which counters "Fear")

d. Willingness to Work (which counters "Laziness")

e. Gratefulness (which counters "Complaining and Criticism")

f. Repentance (which counters "Sins Deceitfulness" and "Callousness/A Hard Heart")

A coaching principle that took me a little bit to buy into was "Whatever we focus on, is what grows in our lives, whether good or bad." It wasn't hard to buy into the positive: if I focus on faith, my faith will grow. If I focus on trust in God, I will grow in trusting God. If I focus on gratefulness, my gratefulness of heart will grow.

But the opposite took a bit of processing on my part, but I came to conclude it , too, was true: if I focus on pride (even in an effort to overcome pride), I will grow in pride, if I focus on fear, my fear will increase, if I focus on complaining and criticism, my critical spirit will increase.

When I focus on anything, that is what I see around me, that is what I recognize in myself and that is what grows.

Therefore, to grow in teachableness, I need to focus not on those things that hinder teachableness, but on their opposites: belief, humility, trust in God, willingness to work, gratefulness and repentance.

5.   Obey what we know God has already taught us or commanded us to do.

This is one of my basic life principles. When people come to me and ask, "How can I know what God's will is for me?" I always respond: "What is the last thing you KNOW God told you to do? Have you completed that? Have you continued to do that? Have you been faithful to that? Keep doing what it is that you know God has told you to do last and you will be in a position for him to show you what (if anything) he wants you to do differently than that."

In the story of Jonah, the boat heading to Tarshish on which Jonah was riding was caught in a huge storm. The ship was threatened with breaking up and even the seasoned sailors onboard were terrified. Each called on his god for deliverance. When they found Jonah asleep, they awakened him and pled with him to join them in praying to his god that they might be saved.

It was only after casting lots to discover the one at fault for bringing this divine storm on them that Jonah's past disobedience was revealed.

All the prayers in the world would not save Jonah and his ship until he was willing to obey the first command that God had given to him: *"Go to the great city of Nineveh and preach against it, because its wickedness has come up before me."* (Jonah 1:2)

The principle is similarly applied to teachability. Has God taught me something that I have not yet applied? Has God commanded me to do something that I have not yet obeyed?

If I desire to be teachable, part of my readiness lies in obeying what God has already told me to do.

6.   Study the Word of God

This may seem like one of those things that shouldn't need to be said, but if you are going to be taught by God, you need to be studying regularly in His Word. That is God's primary teaching for you. Everything else anyone will teach you is supplementary to that. Everything else needs to be held up to the standard of truth that is found in that book. If you don't know it well, you won't be able to know what it is that you are comparing other truth to.

7.   Be open to chastisement.

I don't like this one. We touched on it in the previous chapter when we discussed Peter being confronted by Paul over the issue of eating with Gentile believers when Jewish believers came to town. It is one of the hard ways that God teaches us: "through personal tragedy or failure."

The issue in this chapter is that being open to it is a way that we can grow in being teachable.

The Baker Encyclopedia of the Bible defines "chastisement" as "Correction intended to produce righteousness."[78]

There is chastening that comes from God and chastening that comes from other people (not excluding that often God brings chastening THROUGH other people).

While the theme is found throughout scripture[79], for me the paramount scripture on God's chastening is Hebrews 12:5–11:

And have you completely forgotten this word of encouragement that addresses you as a father addresses his son? It says, "My son, do not make light of the Lord's discipline, and do not lose heart when he rebukes you, because the Lord disciplines the one he loves, and he chastens everyone he accepts as his son." Endure hardship as discipline; God is treating you as his children. For what children are not disciplined by their father? If you are not disciplined—and everyone undergoes discipline—then you are not legitimate, not true sons and daughters at all. Moreover, we have all had human fathers who disciplined us and we respected them for it. How much more should we submit to the Father of spirits and live! They disciplined us for a little while as they thought best; but God disciplines us for our good, in order that we may share in his holiness. No discipline seems pleasant at the time, but painful. Later on, however, it produces a harvest of righteousness and peace for those who have been trained by it.

Chastening by other people is just as painful (and sometimes easier for us to reject) and yet it is one of the ways that God works.

As we have already examined (in ch. 7) God's chastised David through Nathan after David's sin with Bathsheba and Uriah.

In the New Testament we see calls for both private instances of chastening (Matt 18) as well as public instances of chastening (I Cor. 5).

I would make just three comments about chastisement:

1. Chastisement is different from condemnation. As Paul makes abundantly clear in I and II Corinthians, the purpose

of chastisement is repentance and restoration. Its purpose is never to leave the chastened person in a condemned and estranged place. Its purpose is to restore. Now, there are times when repentance and restoration is rejected by the chastened one, but that still must be the intended result.

2.   Chastisement is different from shaming. We have discussed guilt and shame previously. I have proposed that guilt and behavioral shame are based on what you DO. Existential shame is based on who you ARE.

3.   Chastisement has no benefit in alleviating God's anger at our sin, but it is often done so that we may see sin in the same light as does God.

F. B. Meyer says in of *The Way into the Holiest* about chastisement:

Of course we know that the penalty of our sins has been laid on the head of our great Substitute; and that, therefore, we are forever relieved from their penal consequences. But though that is so, yet often chastisement follows on our wrong-doing; not that we expiate the wrong-doing by suffering, but that we may be compelled to regard it in its true light. Amid the pain we suffer we are compelled to review our past. The carelessness, the unwatchfulness, the prayerlessness which have been working within us pass slowly before our minds. We see where we had been going astray for long months or years. We discover how deeply and incessantly we had been grieving God's Holy Spirit. We find that an alienation had been widening the breach between God and our souls, which, if it had proceeded further, must have involved moral ruin. Perhaps we never see our true character until the light dies off the landscape, and the clouds overcast the sky, and the wind rises moaningly about the house of our life.[80]

8. Expect God to teach us through prayer and worship.

When we come face to face with God through prayer and worship, we need to both come with an expectation that God is going to teach us, and also that he wants to increase our desire and ability to be teachable.

What is the role of prayer in readiness (praying for a teachable spirit)? If as has been asserted over and over in this book, God desires for us to have a teachable spirit, then it is fitting that we pray for one.

This may, however, be like the old saying about praying for patience. "Don't what to do it unless you are willing for God to push you into situations that will test and grow your patience."

Likewise, to pray for a teachable spirit is a noble thing and a dangerous thing! As William Saroyan is quoted above, "We get very little wisdom from success."[81] To learn lessons means that we will be pushed and tested and often fail. And none of that feels good.

It is noble, however, because it means we are willing to be used at a deeper level by God. We want to go higher and deeper in the life that he has for us. We want to see the things that others miss. We want to jump on the opportunities that have been hidden from us before.

I am struck by the poster I saw in a classroom one time: "If you are not willing to learn, no one can help you. If you are determined to learn, no one can stop you."

True worship and its elements are highly disparaged today. Instead of expecting God to be present and to speak, we come to be entertained. We come expecting that the preacher will confirm our prejudices by the sermon that he preaches, by the activities that are promoted and by the songs that are sung.

Several months after the fall of Jerusalem in 586 B.C., a messenger arrived in Babylon with the news that the city had fallen.

The night before the messenger arrived, God sent a vision to Ezekiel. He revealed to Ezekiel that the people who remained in conquered Israel were confident that God was going to turn the land over to them. They held that confidence despite the fact that they still worshiped idols, they ate meat with the blood still in it (in violation of Lev. 19:26) and committed acts of violence and sexual immorality (Ezek. 33:23-26) [see above—"Obey what we know God has already taught us or commanded us to do" before expecting God to reveal anything else].

God then went on to tell Ezekiel that while he was popular among the Jewish exiles in Babylon (*"As for you, son of man, your people are talking together about you by the walls and at the doors of the houses, saying to each other, 'Come and hear the message that has come from the LORD.' My people come to you, as they usually do, and sit before you to hear your words…"* Ezek 33:30-31a), the people had no real interest in being teachable and acting on what God was revealing to them: *"Their mouths speak of love, but their hearts are greedy for unjust gain. Indeed, to them you are nothing more than one who sings love songs with a beautiful voice and plays an instrument well, for they hear your words but do not put them into practice."*(Ezek 33:31b-32)

Would that be a description of many churches today? They come to hear movie star musicians and preachers. They come with an attitude of superiority—"I will be the judge of the music and the sermon."

Paul wrote*: "For the time will come when people will not put up with sound doctrine. Instead, to suit their own desires, they will gather around them a great number of teachers to say what their itching ears want to hear."* (2 Tim 4:3)

We come not to be submitted to the Word of God and to learn what God says to us through those who direct the worship services. We come to critique and evaluate. We don't expect that even in a bad sermon or a bad worship music set (they exist!), God can still speak.

We think that we can stay home and read our Bible for ourselves or watch a TV preacher and not miss out on anything that God is wanting to teach us.

Instead, those who are teachable come expecting that God will meet with them there to teach them things that they will miss out on if they are absent. Those who are teachable come expecting that God has been speaking to the one presenting the lesson that morning and that God will either speak through the message of that lesson or in spite of it.

Those who are teachable come expecting that they will learn from those who gather for worship around them. Those who are teachable don't rush in at the last minute and rush out with the last song or prayer. Those who are teachable engage with fellow worshippers believing that God has something to teach them today through those who worship with them each Sunday.

Worship leaders need to be willing to be teachable as they sit under the guidance of the preacher(s) of the church. (We will examine leadership and being teachable below)

9. Practice Judgment-Free Awareness

How many of us have heard comments like this:

- That retreat was a disaster! You have no place in youth ministry!

- That sermon was so bad...why do you even try to preach God's Word?

- You made that family angry when you called on them. You can never be trusted to go and meet with hurting families!

While all of us have heard criticisms, the level of criticism leveled above is so harsh that few of us have heard or would ever give it to another co-worker in the church.

But I suspect that many of us have received an evaluation that somehow resembled the ones I have just given. Was it given by a contrary elder? Not necessarily. Was it given by a disgruntled family over their shoulder as they walked out the door for good? Again, probably not.

In most cases the evaluation was the evaluation we gave to ourselves in looking back on our performance in one role or another.

And what good came of that evaluation?

- Did it help us to objectively identify the things that we could do to improve our level of leadership give in the future? No.

- Did it prompt us to reach to a higher level next time? Not likely.

It simply judged us. It simply held us down. It simply made us LESS confident in our next undertakings in ministry.

Judgment is defined as "the act of assigning a negative or positive value to an event."[82] While critical judgment, may, on a few occasions may have a short-term motivating effect, its long-term effects are always debilitating.

What does self-judgment do?

1. It distracts us

2. Our focus becomes on the failures of the past instead of the potential of the future.

3. Instead of propelling us toward improvement, self-judgment stops us.

A principle that I am working to develop in myself is the concept of "Judgment-free awareness."

The concept of Judgment Free Awareness (JFA) was developed

in the mid-1970s by a tennis coach, Timothy Gallwey. He published his ideas in a little book entitled, *"The Inner Game of Tennis."* The book has become a classic, but not just for tennis.

In 1974, when the book came out, there were not a lot of books on the mental aspects of sports. Most presumed that physical strength, relentless practice and sheer determination was what made the best players.

But from observing what helped his clients improve, tennis pro Timothy Gallwey realized that just as important (even more so in many cases) as skill development was the inner game: the self-talk. He advocated what he called "judgment-free awareness", a technique that allows you to notice what you are doing and how you are doing it without judgmental criticism of yourself.

I believe that the concept of judgment-free awareness can help us not only improve in sports, but to have growing, more effective ministries and live more productive and fulfilling lives.

Gallwey notes that there are two selves within each of us: the teller and the doer. The doer "does" and the teller makes note upon the action. Our doer, then, almost always follows the evaluation given by the teller.

But the teller is not always an accurate guide. Gallwey (p. 35) "First the mind (the teller) judges the event, then groups events, then identifies with the combined event and finally judges itself."

- "You mispronounced that word."

- "You mispronounced another word."

- "You even mispronounced THAT simple word."

THEN,

- "You do not know how to pronounce technical terms correctly."

- "You must be uneducated or stupid."

- "You are no good."

And amazingly the body responds: it seems unable to pronounce any word that at first appears difficult.

Our Christian faith affirms the importance of "the inner game":

- Prov. 23:7: *"For as he thinketh in his heart, so is he."* (KJV)

- Matt 15:19: *"Out of the heart come evil thoughts, murder, adultery, sexual immorality, theft, false testimony, slander."* (Jesus)

Judgment-free awareness is the process of noticing what you are doing and how you are doing it without harsh criticism. Instead the focus is upon observation, so that improvement can be made.

JFA shifts the person from reacting to responding resourcefully in the moment. This allows you to stay fully engaged in what you are doing and focused on your picture of excellence - rather than the "mistakes" you are making right now.

- <u>Not</u>- I wasn't successful at this, I am such a loser.

- <u>But</u>- I wasn't successful at this, that's interesting. What can I do differently next time?

Judgment-free awareness frees me up to come up with options. JFA allows me to move into the future, not just be stuck in the past.

I can either be a loser or a learner.

Whether I succeeded or I failed, what did I learn? Can I learn...

- Something about myself?

- Something about how to improve my skill?

- Something about life?

- Something about the way I played or handled the situation?

Galway uses what I consider to be a profound illustration:

"When we plant a rose seed in the earth, we notice that it is small, but we don't criticize it as "rootless and stemless." We treat it as a seed, giving it the water and nourishment required of a seed. When it first shoots up out of the earth, we don't condemn it as immature and underdeveloped, nor do we criticize the buds for not being open when they appear. We stand in wonder at the process is taking place and give the plant the care it needs at each stage of its development. The rose is a rose from the time it is a seed to the time it dies. Within it at all times, it contains its whole potential. It seems to be constantly in the process of change; yet at each state, at each moment, it is perfectly all right as it is.

"Similarly, the errors we make can be seen as an important part of the developing process. In its process of developing, our tennis game learns a great deal from errors. Even slumps are part of the process. They are not 'bad" events, but they seem to endure endlessly as long as we call them bad & identify with them. Like a good gardener who knows when the soil needs alkaline and when acid, the competent tennis pro should be able to help the development of your game."[83]

Gallwey says, "There is always an inner game being played in your mind, no matter what outer game you are playing. How aware you are of this game can make the difference between success and failure."[84]

The inner game of Christian growth and leadership are no different.

10. Be ruthless in looking for application.

I'm not sure why, but I love trivia. Especially useless trivia. Back when "Trivial Pursuit" first came out, everybody always wanted me on their team, because I knew the most useless information. For example, did you know that…

- Carnivorous animals will not eat another animal that has been hit by a lightning strike.

- A group of geese on the ground is a gaggle, a group of geese in the air is a skein.

- Cats have over one hundred vocal sounds, while dogs only have about ten.

- The housefly hums in the middle octave, key of F.

- The longest recorded flight of a chicken is thirteen seconds.

- A pregnant goldfish is called a twit.

- Armadillos are the only animal besides humans that can get leprosy.

- Twelve or more cows are known as a "flink."

- The pupil of an octopus' eye is rectangular.

- The distance between an alligator's eyes, in inches, is directly proportional to the length of the alligator, in feet.[85]

And what, exactly are you do with that information? Likely nothing. It is pretty useless. Interesting. Fun, perhaps. But useless.

That is not what we are talking about here. If you are going to grow in your teachableness, you MUST learn to apply the information you have.

God does not lead us into situations or into new understandings so we can be the smartest guy or gal in our group. He leads us into situations or understandings because he wants us to apply...to use that knowledge. He invariably puts you in situations that allow you to use those experiences.

In James 1:22-25, the apostle James says: *"Do not merely listen to the word, and so deceive yourselves. Do what it says. Those who listen to the word but do not do what it says are like people who look at their faces in a mirror and, after looking at themselves, go away and immediately forget what they look like.*

But those who look intently into the perfect law that gives freedom and continue in it—not forgetting what they have heard but doing it—they will be blessed in what they do."

John Maxwell quotes Don Shula and Ken Blanchard from *Everyone's a Coach* when they say, "Learning is defined as a change in behavior. You haven't learned a thing until you can take action and use it."[86]

This is especially true of those who teach God's Word. The celebrated preacher Charles Spurgeon said,

> "I am fearful that even preaching against sin may have an injurious effect on the preacher. I frankly confess that there is a tendency with those of us who have to speak on these themes to treat them professionally, rather than to make application of them to ourselves. And thus we lose our dread of evil in some degree, just as young doctors soon lose their tender nervousness in the dissecting room."[87]

In *The Seven Laws of Teaching* that I have referenced before, John Milton Gregory lists four degrees of knowledge:

a. Faint recognition

b. The ability to recall for ourselves

c. The power readily to explain, prove, illustrate, and apply it

d. Such knowledge and appreciation of the truth in its deeper significance and wider relations, that by the force of its importance we act upon it—our conduct is modified by it. (emphasis mine)[88]

I would call the difference between "apply it" in c. and "we act upon it" in d. as "apply it" means we know HOW to apply it. "We act upon it" means we actually do it, and not simply knowing HOW to apply it.

When my wife asked me that simple question, "What has God

taught you?" it confronted me with the fact that I wasn't altogether in a teachable place. After realizing that, the next question I had to ask was, "How can I become more teachable?" Over the past few years I have better learned how to…

1. Look at the big picture.

2. Be willing to fail.

3. Cultivate my listening skills in listening to God and others.

4. Develop those characteristics in my life that are the opposite of those things that hinder teachableness.

5. Obey what I know God has already taught me or commanded me to do.

6. Study the Word of God.

7. Be open to chastisement.

8. Expect God to teach us through prayer and worship.

9. Practice Judgment-Free Awareness.

10. Be ruthless in looking for application.

Chapter 8: Questions for Personal Thought and Group Discussion

- What does "readiness for learning" mean to you?

- For each of the ten ways listed to increase your teachableness, ask : "What has been an instance of you not _____ and thus not learning the lessons that were being presented to you?" How can you think and act differently in the future? Describe how you might be different if you developed these traits in your life.

  - Looking for the big picture.

  - Being willing to fail.

  - Cultivating your listening skills.

  - Developing those characteristics in your life that are the opposite of those things that hinder teachableness.
    - ✓ Belief
    - ✓ Humility
    - ✓ Trust in God
    - ✓ Willingness to Work
    - ✓ Gratefulness
    - ✓ Repentance

  - Obeying what we know God has already taught us or commanded us to do.

- ○ Studying the Word of God.

- ○ Being open to chastisement.

- ○ Expecting God to teach us through prayer and

- ○ worship.

- ○ Developing judgment free awareness in your life.

- ○ Looking ruthlessly for application.

- Where would you place yourself on The Teachability Index? (p. 131) What does that tell you?

- How can you better cultivate your listening skills to be able to better listen..
  - ○ to God

  - ○ to others

Fable #9: Smart Animals, Foolish Group

Lightening had ignited a fire in part of the forest. The animals gathered in a clearing to decide what they should do. The mole who, although he lived underground and was almost blind and deaf with his tiny eyes and ears, was, nevertheless the loudest and most verbose.

"There is nothing to fear!" he loudly declared in a shrill voice. "The fire is far away and there is a stream between us and where the fire is said to be. Nothing to worry about, nothing at all.

The owl thought, "I flew high above and the fire seemed to be coming this way quickly. I fear there are many things to worry about," but because he didn't want to sound pessimistic he said nothing.

The bear thought, "My sense of smell is keen and the smell of smoke keeps getting stronger and stronger. I am not so sure we shouldn't be concerned." But because he thought others probably knew better than he did, the bear kept still.

The bat, meanwhile flitted from branch to branch. She thought, "My hearing tells me that there is a crackling of fire and a falling of trees not far away. I am concerned that we should flee". But out of respect for the mole, she said nothing.

The squirrel, the deer, the porcupine and the fox all had their concerns, but since their brothers and sisters of the forest who could see, hear and smell better than they could seemed not to be concerned, they did not speak up either.

Suddenly the fire burst forth and began to quickly progress across the meadow. The mole quickly dove down it's hole and burrowed deeper to be safe. While the other animals fled, many were burned and others were badly injured.

Moral: Sometimes groups are less intelligent than their individual members.

CHAPTER 9: TEACHABLENESS AND LEADERSHIP

"Leadership and learning are indispensable to each other."

— *John F. Kennedy*
From speech prepared for delivery in Dallas, Texas, November 22, 1963

The article making the news wires had originated on Chaplain.net. It told of the brief interaction between a hospital chaplain and a visiting pastor. Let me quote directly from the article:

> My chaplain's office sits off a well-trafficked hallway inside the VA hospital in Sacramento. A large "Chaplain Service" sign hanging outside the door guides impromptu visitors into the suite.

> Last week, a pastor entered to introduce himself as the spirit-filled "Brother So-and-So." If you are unfamiliar with the adjective "Spirit-filled," it means to embody the spirit of Christ. Or, loosely translated, it's the charismatic next step after "born-again."

> Let me pause a moment to say, I have lots of wonderful charismatic friends. And most of them will tell you that if you are indeed filled with the Spirit, there is no need to self-identify as such. If true, it will be obvious.

> Suffice it to say, I was quickly wishing that Mr. Brother Pastor had kept walking the hall. But instead, the tall, broad and aging pastor sat down and proceeded to recite his resume.

> He talked about the prison ministry he ran and he fed me the details of his meals to the homeless. He buzzed about the radio

preaching he did in Fresno and the television ministry he ran in Bakersfield.

In between each story, he paused to wait for my "amen," but alas, I offered only a polite nod. He talked so long and so fast, I was having trouble hearing the Spirit.

He then shifted the conversation into the many years he served as a pastor and the hospital visitations he did. He confessed that he pitied me because "we both know that government chaplains can't talk about God as freely as a pastor."

And somewhere in the midst of his pontification, he told me that he was praying that God would make him "teachable." If he noticed the smirk that word "teachable" brought to my face, he didn't say.

Instead, he abruptly assumed a crouching position and told me he was going to pray for me. That's when I decided that I'd answer his prayer and offer him a teachable moment.

"Wait just a minute," I said. "How do you know what to pray for?"

"Huh?" he asked.

I asked this because people sometimes offer their prayers, not as a gift, but as a way to establish their power over the pray-ee. My guess was that Pastor Pray4U was going to thank God that I was blessed by his visit today.

I continued. "Well, you mentioned a few minutes ago that you were praying God would make you teachable, so let me share something with you."

He gave me a glassy stare, as clueless as a calf frozen before a new gate.

"When I visit a patient, I always ask them how I can pray for them. I ask them what they want me to pray for. Wouldn't you like to know what you can pray for me?"

With that, God answered his prayer to become teachable and he leaned back in his chair, and spread his hands open on his lap.

"You're right," he said. "What should I pray?"

I asked that he pray for our incoming chaplain supervisor and our new chapel. He agreed with a humble nod. Then I asked him to pray that God would comfort the families of the two hospital employees who'd unexpectedly died the previous week.

He shook his head, still unsure what to say.

He did pray, just not the prayer I'd expected. His prayer was a humble and contrite one asking God for the things we agreed upon. Finally, after he'd said the "amen," he raised his head and I read a "spirit filled" look that indeed told me he just might be teachable.[89]

Of all of those who should be the most teachable, one might think it should be leaders. Most leaders have only gotten to the leadership positions they are in by being teachable.

And yet somewhere between aspiring leader and functioning leader, many have lost their ability to be teachable. Being teachable is an essential characteristic needed in leaders today.

Aaron Story (the lead pastor minister of IndieMetro Church in Indianapolis, IN) has said, "As long as you carry an unteachable demeanor, you will always have a glass ceiling as a leader."[90]

The wisest human leader of them all, Solomon, recognized the importance of being teachable and learning. He began his collection of wisdom proverbs[91]:

The proverbs of Solomon son of David, king of Israel: for gaining wisdom and instruction; for understanding words of insight; for receiving instruction in prudent behavior, doing what is right and just and fair; for giving prudence to those who are simple, knowledge and discretion to the young— let the wise listen and add to their learning, and let the discerning get guidance. (Proverbs 1:1–5)

"Let the wise listen and add to their learning, and let the discerning get guidance." What better word picture is there of a teachable leader?

Being teachable is an essential characteristic of leaders, but it is also the very characteristic which everything around them seems to conspire to drive out of them. Leaders are often very disconnected from those they lead. Those around a leader may simply tell him or her what they believe the leader want to hear, or present the evidence that they know will back up the conclusion the leader prefers.

The tragic story of Rehoboam reminds us of the dangers of losing teachability and instead only listening to those who appeal to our baser nature. Upon Solomon's death, the people urged Solomon's son Rehoboam to lighten the tax burden that Solomon had placed on them to fund the large national and personal expenditures. The older advisers, the ones who had advised his father, counseled him to listen to the people and lighten the tax burden.

But I Kings 12:8 shows Rehoboam's unteachableness: he rejected their advice and sought out those who would support what he already wanted to do: to increase the tax burden, instead of lowering it. The result was tragic. The northern ten tribes gathered around the general Jeroboam and broke away to form a new nation. The divided kingdom was to remain such for centuries.

The same can be said of spiritual leaders today. Teachability is a necessary characteristic of leaders in the church.

In the list of qualification for spiritual leaders given in the pastoral epistles, teachability is found, even though that exact word is not used.

In Titus 1:7 one of the character traits is "not overbearing" (NIV).[92] The Greek word *authadees* is only also found in 2 Peter 2:10

where one of the characteristic of the unrighteous is "arrogant" (ESV-"willful"; KJV-"self-willed").

The Greek translation of the Old Testament (done in the 3rd and 2nd centuries BC) use the word *authadees* to translate the Hebrew in Prov. 21:4 (NIV: *"the arrogant man"*).

"Arrogance", "self-willed", and "selfish" all seem to be the opposite of teachable. These are things which the Christian leader must not be.

Another interesting qualification of spiritual leaders related to teachableness is found in I Tim. 3.2 and 2 Tim 2:24. The words used in these two places are similar. I Tim 3:2 uses the Greek word *didaktikos* and 2 Tim 2:24 uses the similar word *didaktos*. While the word is usually translated in these passages as "able to teach", it can have the sense of "able to be taught." That sense is definitely the sense in which that word is used in John 6:45 where the people of God will *"all be taught"* (NIV) by Him.

In fact, the ISV (International Standard Version) translates *didaktikon* and *didaktos* as "teachable" in both I Tim. 3.2 and 2 Tim 2:24:

I Tim 3:2: *"Therefore, an elder must be blameless, the husband of one wife, stable, sensible, respectable, a lover of strangers, and teachable."*

2 Tim 2:24: *"A servant of the Lord must not argue. Instead, he must be kind to everyone, teachable, willing to suffer wrong."*[93]

That "teachable" is at least one legitimate way to translate these words is reinforced by the fact that the early Christian leader Cyprian, in his *Epistle To Pompey, Against the Epistle of Stephen About the Baptism of Heretics (Epistle 73)* translates these words in this way:

"Apostle Paul writes to Timothy, and warns him that a bishop must not be "litigious, nor contentious, but gentle and teachable." [Latin: docibilis] Now he is teachable who is meek and gentle to the patience of learning. For it behooves a bishop not only to teach, but also to learn; because he also teaches better who daily increases and advances by learning better; which very thing, moreover, the same Apostle Paul teaches, when he admonishes, "that if anything better be revealed to one sitting by, the first should hold his peace."[94]

Later on, Augustine in his *Writings against the Manichaeans and against the Donatists* uses the same argument (including many of the same exact words) when referring to the same verse, he says:

> To go on to what he says, "that a bishop should be 'teachable,'" adding, "But he is teachable who is gentle and meek to learn; for a bishop ought not only to teach, but to learn as well, since he is indeed the better teacher who daily grows and advances by learning better things;"[95]

Whichever Paul's foremost sense in his use of the word "*didaktos*", I believe it is fair to say that there is an inseparable link between being able to teach, and being teachable.

Eli Cohen and Noel Tichy note in an article in the professional journal of the American Society for Training and Development that the link between teaching and being teachable is solidly exhibited in many of the strongest companies of America:

> **To develop others, leaders must have a teachable point of view**[96]. A teachable point of view is a leader's opinion on what it takes to win in his or her business and what it takes to lead other people. In the companies we studied we observed that acquiring a teachable point of view involved in-depth preparation by the leaders. Once they had a teachable point of view, they thought of creative ways to find teaching and learning opportunities. They tried to turn every interaction with their people into a learning and teaching event and often set aside time to teach leadership outside of scheduled activities.[97]

And yet all of us could point to leaders, religious and secular, who exhibit no signs of teachability whatsoever.

Early on in ministry I worked with a ministry leader who was unteachable. He was handsome, athletic and charismatic. I believe that he thought he was teachable. He went to a lot of church growth seminars and grabbed the latest idea to come down the street from the church growth gurus of the day. He thought he was teachable, because he would adapt ideas from these large church leaders. But he wasn't really teachable at all. These ideas became HIS ideas only to fulfill his agenda which was set in stone. There was no aspect of church life at which he did not believe he was the best. His preaching was "the best around." His interpersonal skills "couldn't be better." His leadership skills "par excellence". His business acumen: "sterling". (He once took me shopping before an important church leadership board meeting at which he was going to buy a new "power suit." He bought a new suit before every important meeting or church holiday. [What he did with them all, I never knew]. He was going to overwhelm the opposition on the board by his clothing and style.) He hobnobbed with the wealthier members of the congregation and was only interested in what would advance his career in ministry.

He eventually left in a hurry after a hush-hush scandal and I have never heard from him since. My wife says, "If you ever have to make a decision about whether something in ministry is right or wrong, just imagine what [Harry] would do…and do the opposite. That way you know you'll be doing the right thing."

Harsh. But pretty accurate. The unteachable leader will not be taught, and ultimately he has nothing positive to teach.

Why are some Christian leaders (groups in particular) teachable and others not?

I would identify nine reasons (there are certainly more):

1. Image-consciousness

We live in an image conscious…no…image **obsessed** culture. From the way that you dress to your image reflected in social media, image drives much of our world.

Time and time again, I heard in the church that we needed to be careful of our image as leaders with the congregation or our image as leaders of our church in the community. And to a degree, that may be true, but too often leaders are so obsessed with image that it affects us doing what is right.   To admit that we don't always have all the answers or always have our act together is perceived, too often, as "unleadership-like". Image can take precedence over character and growth.

Who were the most image conscious people in the New Testament?   The Pharisees. Jesus soundly and regularly condemned their image consciousness:

> Matt 23:25-28: *"Woe to you, teachers of the law and Pharisees, you hypocrites! You clean the outside of the cup and dish, but inside they are full of greed and self-indulgence. Blind Pharisee! First clean the inside of the cup and dish, and then the outside also will be clean.*
>
> *"Woe to you, teachers of the law and Pharisees, you hypocrites! You are like whitewashed tombs, which look beautiful on the outside but on the inside are full of the bones of the dead and everything unclean. In the same way, on the outside you appear to people as righteous but on the inside you are full of hypocrisy and wickedness."*

The issue for Jesus was not what they looked like on the outside—their image. It was who they were inside.

2. Too much reliance on education or experience

You will not find me giving diatribes against education. I have always appreciated the words of former Harvard president Derek Bok: ""If you think education is expensive, try ignorance."

I come from a multi-generation family of educators. If it were up to me, John Wesley would have added "Learn all you can" to his famous maxim: "Earn all you can, save all you can, give all you can."

But we must know the proper place of formal education. It is critical in the preparation (and continuing preparation) stage. But it never must be a substitute for being teachable in the moment.

When I am talking with men and women who say they don't believe in God, I ask them to draw a circle on a piece of paper. I state, "This circle represents all possible human knowledge....past, present and future." Then I ask then to draw another circle within that representing how much of that knowledge they have. (I prompt them; "Half? A quarter? An eighth?") Most respond either with the smallest circle they can draw or just putting a dot somewhere in the bigger circle. I then ask, "Is it possible that the existence and character of God is somewhere outside of that dot of knowledge and understanding that you have?

It serves us all well to be a little more humble. I often want to draw my "knowledge circle" and ask leaders how much of that knowledge they have. The follow-up questions is something like "Is it possible that the answer to this question or the solution to our problem might (conceivably) be outside of your small knowledge of education and experience?"

Most of us have known men and women fresh out of high school, or college or graduate school. They say they are "done" with education. There is nothing more that they need to learn to live life. But meet them five years or so later after life has thrown them around a bit and their story is often very different.

Leaders who rely on their degrees or their past successes can be tempted to be unteachable.

Jesus referred to this, I believe when he spoke harshly at the Jewish leaders of his day: *"You search the scriptures because you think that in them you have eternal life; and it is they that testify on my behalf."* (John

5.39)

They were so proud of how much they knew (or thought that they knew). In reality, it kept them from learning from the one who was the author of the scriptures they studied.

3. Isolation

The phrase "It's lonely at the top" is a maxim of leadership. But it doesn't have to be. Anyone who has served in leadership responsibilities for any length of time has felt the pressure that comes when making hard decisions comes down to you. A decision could go one way or another and basically you have to decide. These don't usually seem to be insignificant matters.

But it is possible also for a leader to either not open themselves up to input from others, or for subordinates to fear bringing bad news or a dissenting voice.

The Proverb that I have quoted elsewhere *"In the multitude of counselors there is safety."* (Prov 11:14, NKJV) is true. When the leader is isolated from other voices, particularly dissenting voices, bad decisions inevitably are the result. We do not show teachableness when we isolate ourselves from those under or around us.

This danger doesn't exist only in the church. An article published in *Homeland Security Affairs Journal* noted instances where time and time again isolation proved harmful either in response to emergencies or for the common good. Whether it was the response to Hurricane Katrina in 2005, the attacks on Sept. 11, 2001, the Oklahoma City bombing in 1995 or Hurricane Andrew in 1992 (to name just a few) isolation kept leaders from making the best choices in the situation.

The study referenced above, noted,

Generally, every discipline does their own form of ICS [Incident Command System] training and agencies train in isolation. Often this training is too simplistic to delve into the subtle skills of disciplined, team-based, decision making. Further, responders cannot be expected to learn the functions of incident management in the heat of an event. As one captain told us, "You can't grab 'regular' police officers and firefighters and take them away from handling the stuff they're handling to do incident management stuff. If they haven't already been training in logistics, it will take them a long time to figure it out, and they have other things to be worrying about." Yet, absent sound training, this is exactly what happens, with the needless result that recognized and well-developed incident management functions are carried out poorly.[98]

There is also the isolation that arises from minimizing or marginalizing certain groups in the church. Jesus' disciples seemed particularly susceptible to this. In Matthew 15:21-28, a Syrophoenician woman sought after Jesus.[99] The disciples came to Jesus seeking to have him send her away since she was making a ruckus in her attempts to see Jesus. She was not "politically correct" and so the disciples did not want Jesus to bother with her.

Another example would be the refusal of the disciples to allow parents who had brought their children to Jesus in order that he may bless them. The disciples barred the way and scolded the parents for trying to bring such unimportant people to Jesus

In both cases, the subject was not considered "worthy" by the disciples of Jesus' attention.

Tragically, it is easy for leaders, Christian or not, to discount the concerns or suggestions of those people who either are not influential or powerful in the church, or those who cannot contribute a lot to the church (whether financially or in time and service).

This becomes especially problematic when the person is considered a troublemaker or squeaky wheel in the organization. (This is one of the problems of always being a complainer). It is easy for leaders to ignore the suggestions or questions of a troublemaker, dismissing them because of the source.

Teachable leaders will not only be open to the views of the disenfranchised in their circle of leadership, but they will seek them out. That doesn't necessarily mean that you have to respond to every gripe brought by every squeaky wheel. But you must not allow the complaint to be automatically dismissed because of its source.

4. Fear/Insecurity

We dealt with Fear when we discussed the "10 Hindrances to Teachability". But leaders grapple with fear as well. The message of Jesus created a lot of direct and indirect fear within many who heard him, including fear within the Jewish leaders.

> John 12:42–43: *Nevertheless, many even of the authorities believed in him, but for fear of the Pharisees they did not confess it, so that they would not be put out of the synagogue; for they loved the glory that comes from man more than the glory that comes from God.*

> John 3:1-3: *Now there was a man of the Pharisees named Nicodemus, a ruler of the Jews. This man came to Jesus by night and said to him, "Rabbi, we know that you are a teacher come from God, for no one can do these signs that you do unless God is with him." Jesus answered him, "Truly, truly, I say to you, unless one is born again he cannot see the kingdom of God."*

> John 19:38: *After these things Joseph of Arimathea, who was a disciple of Jesus, but secretly for fear of the Jews, asked Pilate that he might take away the body of Jesus, and Pilate gave him permission. So he came and took away his body.*

It was fear that led the unbelieving Jewish leaders to plot the death of Jesus. But it was fear of many of the believing Jewish leaders that kept them from speaking out.

Leaders today, believing and unbelieving, grapple with fear just like those of old. Sometimes it is the fear is of losing one's position. Sometimes it is a fear of the very people they lead. Sometimes it is fear of being identified with other church groups (whether that be Pentecostals, Catholics, Baptists, Fundamentalists, and Liberals, whatever.) Whatever group is looked down upon come to be despised by the group of churches with which this particular church identifies, and thus there can be fear of being identified with them. ("Your worship is too free", "your worship is too liturgical", "only liberals believe that," "I can't believe you find the article by that person helpful. Don't you know he's a raving fundamentalist?") You get my point.

5.   Repeatedly reacting to the same situation/similar situations instead of acting proactively.

When we read the story of Samson in the Old Testament book of Judges, many of us feel pretty good about ourselves.

Here was a man who was powerful enough to be considered a judge over Israel and who led Israel for twenty years (Judges 15.20), and yet a man who had a total lack of self-control when it came to women.

His first Philistine wife wore him down by pouting so that he would give her the answer to a riddle about a lion and honey so she could secretly pass it on to her people and make him lose his bet with them (Judges 14:10-19).

Later he took as his mistress a woman named Delilah. When she was approached by the Philistines and bribed for finding out the source of Samson's great strength, Delilah sought four times to find out the source of His strength so that she could deliver him weak and helpless to the Philistines. The first three times, Samson gives a false reason for his strength. Each time, she had men hidden who then jumped and tried to enslave him. Samson overcame the attackers each time. And Samson kept giving her answers. Finally the fourth time, he gave the real reason (his hair had never been cut) and after she cut it while he slept he was helpless when the same group of men jumped out and tied him up and took him as a slave.

How often do leaders see a similar situation and try the same solution that has failed numerous times before. They think,., "surely this time it will work!"

6.   Weariness/Laziness

The classic example of weariness in scripture is Elijah. His conflict with King Ahab had gone on for several years. Ahab's father, Omri, had allowed temples to the Caananite god Baal to be erected. Omri also arranged for his son Ahab to marry Jezebel, the daughter of the king of Sidon of Phoenicia, who was in her own right a priestess of Baal.

When Ahab ascended the throne he and Jezebel continued the development of the worship of Baal. At first Elijah appeared before the king and declared that a severe drought would come on the nation of Israel in judgment. The drought began. After three years Elijah returns to Ahab and declares an end to the drought.

Elijah and Ahab have a confrontation on Mt. Carmel over which god is real: Baal or Jehovah. In this classic story, the priests of Baal dance and self-mutilate for hours, to no avail. But when it is Elijah's turn, he pours water over the sacrifices to make it harder for it to burn. He prays a simple prayer and fire comes down from heaven consuming the water, the sacrifice, even the stone altar. Elijah calls for the death of the priests of Baal and for the drought to end. And the drought ends.

Enraged by Elijah's order for the deaths of her priests, Jezebel determines to kill Elijah. Out of fear of her, Elijah flees to Beersheba in Judah and finally into the desert. There, after praying for God to kill him, God instead sends an angel to provide food and water for him. Elijah sleeps again and again the angel appears to provide provision for the prophet. .

Elijah traveled for 40 days and 40 nights to Mt. Horeb, the place where the people of Israel had received the Word of the Lord. At Horeb, Elijah hides in a cave. While there, God appears to him and asks, "What are you doing here Elijah?"

> [Elijah] replied, *"I have been very zealous for the LORD God Almighty. The Israelites have rejected your covenant, torn down your altars, and put your prophets to death with the sword. I am the only one left, and now they are trying to kill me too."* (I Kings 19:9b-10)

Elijah was weary. Weariness is the state of physical, emotional, and spiritual depletion. In spite of having witnessed the power, the protection and the provision of God, Elijah was weary. And weariness blinds us. Weariness makes us afraid and lonely. Weariness undermines our dreams, kills our creativity and diminishes our impact.

Instead of us being empowered by teachableness we are in enslaved in reaction mode. John E. Michel puts it this way in an article, "The Weary Leader":

> The danger of all this is that, instead of recognizing how experimenting, failing, falling, and starting again (only smarter), is what equips us to become better tomorrow than we may have been today, weariness convinces us to resist change. The more we resist, the more we stagnate. The more we stagnate, the greater the opportunity for the energy stealing, resentment building effects of weariness to set in and undermine the important contribution we have to make to the world.[100]

There is a lot of bluff and bluster about weariness, causing guilt among leaders. Former Secretary of State Condaleeza Rice told the National Republican Congressional Committee's annual dinner in March 2014 in Washington, D.C. that "Leaders can't afford to grow weary."[101]

Another writer, a pastor's wife writing to other pastor's wives suggest that the women stuff their emotions and pretend nothing is wrong, ""No matter what happens…you walk into that church, hold your head high, and act like nothin's wrong!"

The problem with that advice is that it is incomplete at best and destructive and duplicitous at worst. Weariness must be addressed head on, with self-care, seeking support and understanding, and setting clear boundaries.

7.   Disbelief/carnality

What I am talking about here is not the type of disbelief of atheists and those who despise God. When I am talking about leaders in this chapter, I am mostly talking about Christian leaders…those who claim to follow Christ, but whose behavior really displays little practical belief in his current leadership and activity.

The *New International Encyclopedia of the Bible* defines carnal as

…in an ethical sense, mere human nature, the lower side of man as apart from the Divine influence, and therefore estranged from God and prone to sin; whatever in the soul is weak and tends toward ungodliness.[102]

In other words, it is relying on human knowledge and strength rather than divine knowledge and strength.   It can be observed in such leadership phrases as, "I know that's what the Bible says, but in the REAL world…" or "That's all well and good, but this is a BUSINESS matter."   Or "Preacher, you just take care of people's souls and we will get this church up to where it needs to be…"

I am profoundly struck by the example of Nebuchadnezzar. He was king of the most powerful nation on earth. He is known as the king under whose direction was built one of the Seven Wonders of the Ancient World: the Hanging Gardens of Babylon. His father, Nabopolassar, liberated Babylon from its servitude to Assyria, after the death of the last powerful Assyrian king, Ashurbanipal, destroying Nineveh in the process. (Why couldn't those Babylonians pick simple names like Joe or Dave or Bill?) Nebuchadnezzar was a warrior prince and led his father's troops in battle. After the remnants of the Assyrian government tried to reestablish a capital, in Harran, he captured that city. When they then tried to establish a new capital in Carchemish on the Euphrates, their ally, Egypt marched up to help the Assyrians against Babylon. The Assyrians were again defeated by the Babylonians at the Battle of Carchemish.

Upon his father's death, Nebuchadnezzar returned to Babylon to take his place. His name was a prayer for his success as a ruler. It included the name of the Babylonian god Nabu. His name literally meant, "Oh god Nabu, save my first-born son." He was Nebuchadnezzar.

Nebuchadnezzar is a prominent figure in the latter parts of the Old Testament, particularly in the books of Daniel and Jeremiah. He is the king under which Judah finally fell in 586 B.C. and thereafter he destroyed Solomon's temple, leveled the city and deported most of the citizens to Babylon.

He is also famous for three stories, recorded in Daniel chapters 2, 3, and 4.

In Daniel 2, we read the story of Nebuchadnezzar dreaming of an enormous statue of himself. It was made of varying materials: gold, silver, bronze, iron and clay. The prophet Daniel interpreted the dream as a prediction of the rise and fall of various world empires.

The second story is also in Daniel 2, where we read that Nebuchadnezzar actually constructed that large statue (although it is not clear whether or not the statue was of himself). The law of the land was that when the people heard *"the sound of the horn, flute, zither, lyre, harp, pipe and all kinds of music"* everyone was to fall down and worship the image. (Dan. 3:5).

Three associates of Daniel (Shadrach, Meshach and Abednego) refused to bow down in worship and because of that they were thrown into "a blazing furnace." As most Sunday school children (and fans of the Statler Brothers) know, when Nebuchadnezzar threw them into the furnace,

> *They wouldn't Bend: They held onto the Will of God so we are told*
> *They wouldn't Bow: They wouldn't bow their knees to the idol made of gold*
> *They wouldn't Burn: They were protected by the fourth man in the fire.*
> *They wouldn't Bend, They wouldn't Bow, They wouldn't Burn.*[103]

The third story (Daniel 4) is really the point where the subject of teachability comes into play. The story is unique because it is written in the first person narrative of King Nebuchadnezzar himself. The story is striking because of his opening words; this man who had been victorious in battle (including destroying the temple of the Hebrew God) said:

> *It is my pleasure to tell you about the miraculous signs and wonders that the Most High God has performed for me. How great are his signs, how mighty his wonders! His kingdom is an eternal kingdom; his dominion endures from generation to generation.* (Daniel 4:2–3)

Amazing words coming from the one who was one of the, if not THE, most powerful men in the world. And that was part of the problem. In Daniel's words, *"You [Nebuchadnezzar] have become great and strong; your greatness has grown until it reaches the sky, and your dominion extends to distant parts of the earth."* (Daniel 4:22)

Nebuchadnezzar begins to tell an account of an amazing time in his life. It began with a dream. A dream of a tremendous tree. Nebuchadnezzar describes it this way:

> *before me stood a tree in the middle of the land. Its height was enormous. The tree grew large and strong and its top touched the sky; it was visible to the ends of the earth. Its leaves were beautiful, its fruit abundant, and on it was food for all. Under it the wild animals found shelter, and the birds lived in its branches; from it every creature was fed.* (Daniel. 4:10b-12)

But in the dream, an angel descended and commanded that the tree be cut down. It was to be scattered, leaving only "the stump and roots, bound with iron and bronze, remain[ing] in the ground."

The stump (Note: now referred to as "he" instead of "it") was to remain watered by the dew for seven times and that "he" was to: *"live with the animals among the plants of the earth. Let his mind be changed from that of a human being and let him be given the mind of an animal, till seven times pass by for him."* (Daniel 4:15b-16)

Daniel interpreted the dream to mean that the king would be the one who would wander and live as an animal in the wild for seven years before returning to his glory.

Nebuchadnezzar had forgotten that the source of all people's strength, power, and position is ultimately God himself. And God wanted this pagan king to understand this lesson. He evidently had not learned it when Daniel interpreted the dream of the great statue made of gold, silver, bronze, iron and clay. He evidently had not learned this lesson when God protected Shadrach, Meshach and Abednego in the fiery furnace. He evidently had not even learned it when Daniel interpreted another dream of the king's and predicted the very events that were about to transpire. (Dan. 4-27). To emphasize that this is a lesson in teachableness, Daniel ends his interpretation with a warning: *"Therefore, Your Majesty, be pleased to accept my advice: Renounce your sins by doing what is right, and your wickedness by being kind to the oppressed. It may be that then your prosperity will continue."* (Daniel 4:27).

But Nebuchadnezzar was not yet teachable. For, in the very next verses it states: *"Twelve months later, as the king was walking on the roof of the royal palace of Babylon, he said, "Is not this the great Babylon I have built as the royal residence, by my mighty power and for the glory of my majesty?"* (Daniel 4:29–30)

He was a great leader, but his carnality stood between him and God. He was accustomed to doing this his way…the world's way. And so his dream came to fruition: Nebuchadnezzar, the most powerful man in the world lost his mind. He became as a wild animal and lived in the woods and fields eating grass like livestock. His hair grew long like *"the feathers of an eagle"* and his untrimmed nails grew *"like the claws of a bird."* (Dan. 4:23)

At the end of those seven years, King Nebuchadnezzar was restored in mind, body and position. He lost his carnality and pride and understood what it meant to be teachable. He had learned the lessons that God wanted him to learn:

> *At the end of that time, I, Nebuchadnezzar, raised my eyes toward heaven, and my sanity was restored. Then I praised the Most High; I honored and glorified him who lives forever. His dominion is an eternal dominion; his kingdom endures from generation to generation. All the peoples of the earth are regarded as nothing. He does as he pleases with the powers of heaven and the peoples of the earth. No one can hold back his hand or say to him: "What have you done?"* (Dan 4:34-35)

In a final word, the king writes, *"Now I, Nebuchadnezzar, praise and exalt and glorify the King of heaven, because everything he does is right and all his ways are just. And those who walk in pride he is able to humble."* (Daniel 4:37)

Nebuchadnezzar had become teachable.

I am often known in the circles in which I run as a contrarian. (And, I admit, they don't accuse me of that without some justification!) And so, it is easy to bash an image mentality. In our world's eye, (the carnal eye) image is more important than reality. (That harkens back to the preacher's wife's advice mentioned above: "No matter what happens…you walk into that church, hold your head high, and act like nothin's wrong!")

So in that contrarian spirit I want to say that image IS critically important.

Image MUST drive who we are. The issue relates to carnality of disbelief when we ask, "in whose image are we trying to remake ourselves?"   The issue is not "Should we be concerned with image?" The concern is "In what image [or more properly…'In whose image'] should Church leaders be trying to be made?"

Paul Chappell is the pastor of Lancaster Baptist Church (Lancaster, CA) and the founder of West Coast Baptist College. Chappell gives "20 Characteristics of a Christ-Like Leader".[104] Let me share my adaptation of fifteen of those that I think are most pertinent to this topic:

A leader who is fashioned in the image of Jesus Christ will:

1. Be willing to deny himself/herself.

2. Be submissive to and filled with the Holy Spirit of God.

3. Possess and practice discipline in his life.

4. Read the Word of God and good books consistently.

5. Seek, ask for, and use God's wisdom.

6. Be sincere and deeply caring.

7. Know how to forgive.

8. Find his acceptance in his/her relationship to God the Father.

9. Pray for others.

10. Help others succeed.

11. Know the difference between ambition and vision and is able to articulate vision.

12. Possess a sense of urgency for God's work.

13. Stand on strong convictions.

14. Be kind.

15. Love his/her family.

Carnality is finding any other image than Christ to pattern ourselves after. Whether it be the world's ways or just "I've got to be me," any leadership style that models anything other than obedience to Christ in every aspect of life is carnal.

8.   Only willing to look at one aspect of sacred cow doctrines.

As someone who teaches eastern religions, I am very aware of the meaning of the word "sacred cow." In Hinduism the cow is a very sacred animal. While devout Hindus will not kill most animals, the cow is special. The origins of its sacredness are buried in the fog of pre-history, but it could be that it arises from the pre-Vedic worship of the cow as a symbol of fertility and provision. It also is connected with the belief that as long as one has a cow, one will have "milk and butter, fuel (dried dung to burn), and the warmth and comfort associated with household pets. With a cow, one is never utterly destitute."[105]   The cow is not to be killed in many parts of India, and can basically wander wherever it wants to go.

But the attitude that there are certain things that are off-limits for consideration is not limited to Hinduism. They can be practices or beliefs. They can be as blatant as a picture that cannot be removed because of the person who donated it or the conviction that everything should be done by a majority vote or as subtle as taking good and true doctrines and raising them above all other Christian teaching or bending all other Christian teaching so that it fits in with our preconceptions of one particular doctrine.

It is not just that progress doesn't happen, but leaders become unteachable when we have sacred cows. New lessons that we need to learn can't be learned because we are limited by the sacred cow. Ironically, it is not just "traditionalists" who have sacred cows. In many places the desire to be hip and contemporary means that we exclude practices that are incredibly helpful and have proven themselves to be that way for generations, even centuries. But because it has been used in times past, it is off-limits. That is as much of a sacred cow as the color of the carpets (or having carpets altogether!)

9.   They are willing victims of group-think.

Are we as leaders teachable about the RIGHT THINGS? Who is asking "What is God trying to teach us? How do we know? Are we sure?"

One of the dangers of teachableness is teachable blindness. We think we are teachable because we are open to learning things that benefit us, but deaf to the lessons that make us more uncomfortable.

We want our church to grow, we want income to increase, we want to expand our influence for Christ. And so we look at what others are doing and learn principles and practices that others have found to be successful.

We are not holding on to old ways. We are learning new things. We are teachable. We are pleased with ourselves and making progress toward the goals that we want to reach.

But how do we know that we are actually learning the lessons that God wants us to learn?

Many of us are familiar with the phenomenon of "groupthink." While it did not begin in that year, I was surprised to know that the concept was only coined in 1972.[106] It was very similar to George Orwell's concept of "doublethink" that he described in his novel *1984*.

In 1972, Irving Janis researched and popularized the phrase to describe a specific phenomenon that he observed in World War II infantrymen in combat. He defined "groupthink" as "a mode of thinking that people engage in when they are deeply involved in a cohesive in-group, when the members' strivings for unanimity override their motivation to realistically appraise alternative courses of action."

I like the description of Groupthink that says,

"Groupthink, a term coined by social psychologist Irving Janis (1972), occurs when a group makes faulty decisions because group pressures lead to a deterioration of "mental efficiency, reality testing, and moral judgment. Groups affected by groupthink ignore alternatives and tend to take irrational actions that dehumanize other groups. A group is especially vulnerable to groupthink when its members are similar in background, when the group is insulated from outside opinions, and when there are no clear rules for decision making."[107]

Tragically, examples of group think abound in history: the Bay of Pigs Invasion in 1961, the Challenger Disaster in 1986, the attack on Pearl Harbor in 1941, the military invasion of Iraq in 2003, the collapse of SwissAir in 2001, the mass resignation of the Major League Umpires Association in 1999.

Many groups are enamored with the idea of consensus: the group will not move forward until all members are in agreement on a decision. And this actually can be an antidote for groupthink—that is, if all members feel safe in sharing their concerns and ideas. Often, however, a desire for unity and a desire to reach consensus results in members holding back what concerns they have and the group-think mentality prevailing.

Several years ago I was in a leadership meeting discussing whether a certain staff person should be let go. There had been multiple warnings and the staff person was already on a plan of remediation but had not shown progress in the allotted time. The group consensus was that, even though the staff person was currently on vacation, he should be let go immediately.

One member who was close to the staff person sat noticeably quiet during the discussion. When asked for his contribution, he simply shrugged and said, "Do what you're going to do anyway." He refused to say more.

The staff person was let go and it caused great difficulty in the organization. He should have been let go, but not in the manner that was decided.

Shortly after the staff person was released, the board member began to talk to whoever would listen that he had known, that this way of doing it was not correct.

I confronted the leader and tried to impress upon him that he had not done his job. He was a leader in the organization and he had denied us the value of his perspective. Would the final decision have changed? No. Would the manner in which it was handled have differed? Very possibly. (Regardless of whether or not the group would have listened to his input, his complaining about the decision of the group without contributing his concerns and insights was extremely inappropriate).

CONCLUSION

Leadership and teachability are, in many ways, coterminous. The truly teachable person will eventually begin to be drawn upon by others in a leadership capacity. Any leader who ceases to learn, at that moment begins to forfeit his/her leadership.

In Zechariah chapter 1, Zechariah begins his declaration of God's Word to the people of Israel. They have returned in Palestine after the exile and have resettled the land, especially around Jerusalem. They have built themselves great homes.

But the temple of God lays unfinished. Both Haggai and Zechariah declare God's word to the people of Israel about the necessity of rebuilding the temple, but whereas Haggai's is down to earth with practicalities, Zechariah's message consists of ten apocalyptic visions.

The visions are prefaced, however, with a warning of Zechariah and it is all about leaders and teachability:

"the word of the LORD came to the prophet Zechariah…: "The LORD was very angry with your ancestors. Therefore tell the people: This is what the LORD Almighty says: 'Return to me,' declares the LORD Almighty, 'and

I will return to you,' says the LORD Almighty.

"Do not be like your ancestors, to whom the earlier prophets proclaimed: This is what the LORD Almighty says: 'Turn from your evil ways and your evil practices.' But they would not listen or pay attention to me, declares the LORD. Where are your ancestors now? And the prophets, do they live forever? But did not my words and my decrees, which I commanded my servants the prophets, overtake your ancestors?

"Then they repented and said, 'The LORD Almighty has done to us what our ways and practices deserve, just as he determined to do.'"

I really appreciate John Maxwell's outline of this passage in *The Leadership Bible.* He states, "We must keep learning or we will stop leading. We cannot afford to stagnate, for our world and our people are changing too quickly. New insights and new opportunities appear all the time."

Taking this passage In Zechariah 1, Maxwell provides the following outline of the sources of the leader's learning:[108]

1. **The Past** –Israel's previous years were to warn future generations.

2. **The Prophets** –These men of God spoke God's word and cautioned Israel to listen.

3. **The People** - The people repeatedly failed to repent, and felt miserable.

4. **The Problems** –Trials served to punish the people for disobedience.

5. **The Present** –Zechariah found himself in a similar predicament.

6. **The Principles of God** –God's truth cried out to Zechariah's generation.

May we learn from the example of these and other leaders so that we do not repeat their mistakes.

Chapter 9: Questions for Personal Thought and Group Discussion

- What events do you think happen between "aspiring leader" and "functioning leader" that tempt leaders to give up some of their teachableness?

- What was sparked within you when you read that a legitimate way to translate I Timothy 3:2 and 2 Timothy 2:24 is that a leader (rather than simply "able to teach") must be "teachable"? What difference might that make in leaders?

- If you are a leader, how have you seen your teachableness negatively impacted by:
  - Image consciousness

  - Too much reliance on education or experience.

  - Isolation.

  - Fear/Insecurity.

  - Repeatedly reacting to the same situation/similar situations instead of acting proactively.

  - Weariness/Laziness.

- o   Disbelief/Carnality.

- o   Only willing to look at one aspect of sacred cow doctrines.

- o   Being a willing victim of group-think.

- How can you and those in your leadership circle seek to overcome these negative behaviors?

CHAPTER 10: CONCLUSION

I began this book with a brief explanation of its genesis: my wife's question, "So what has God taught you in this past six months?"

In asking that question, while we knew that I was on a journey, little did either of us know that I was not even in the middle of the journey. I was near the beginning point of the crucible of the lessons that God was teaching me.

The journey continues even to this day. I am releasing these reflections for publication not because I think I have learned all the lessons God has for me, but (frankly) so that I can move on to other writing projects and get feedback from the public generally on my thinking to this point.

In the first draft of this book, I included a long biography of my life that led up to and beyond that day when my wife asked her question. I deleted almost all of that, except for a few examples I have sprinkled throughout the book. There were a couple of reasons for that. One, not everything about my life needs to be told even if it could be and there are others who are a part of my journey who would be unnecessarily hurt if I described the entire journey. Second, the chapter "My Journey: Through the Valley of the Shadow of Death" was fairly dramatic and really could have overshadowed the point of the book. The book isn't about me. It is about being teachable.

But I think it is important in the name of integrity that I share some of the lessons I have gained from this journey. There are many lessons, some of them don't need to be shared publicly, and many of them are not yet finished. But this has been anything but an intellectual exercise for me. So what did I learn? Here are a few lessons learned:

1. My character is the main qualification that I have for ministry. This was a lesson that I had known cognitively for decades, but had not learned to live experientially… therefore I hadn't really learned it.

2. Sin, both my own, and sin that others perpetrate on you, has consequence that last a lifetime, or at least until they are dealt with. In many cases, even after they are "dealt with" there are long-lasting, perhaps permanent consequences.

3. Human Christian leaders are exactly that. They are *leaders* and I am called to respect them for that. They are *Christian*: just because I disagree (even profoundly disagree) with decisions, I have no right to question their commitment to Christ. Third, they are *human*. That both means that they are created in the image of the eternal, creative God, and it means that they are not as wise, powerful or purely-motived as is God. They will make mistakes. There is not a leader alive who will not make profound mistakes. They make them because they are human. They will hurt others. Usually they will not intend to hurt others…but hurt them they will. That, however, does not negate the first two truths…that they are Christian…and they are leaders.

4. Ministry is not what I do…it's who I am. I minister not because I receive a paycheck and can exert leadership in a congregation. Neither of those are true for me currently, but God continues to open doors of ministry to me not because of my position, but because of how he has fashioned me.

5. I am married to an amazing woman. A woman who brings her own baggage to the relationship, but who is stronger

and who has more love to give than I ever gave her credit for.

There are more lessons I have learned, lessons I am learning and more lessons for me to learn, but as I have said, MY lessons are not the main point of this book.

- The point of this book is: are YOU teachable?

- What does being teachable look like for you in your life?

- What lessons has God been trying to teach you that you have resisted learning?

- What does the fact that God has unique lessons for you to learn say about His relationship to you?

- What actions in your life, what attitudes in your life, what beliefs in your life are keeping you from being teachable?

My blessings on you as you continue on this journey of learning to live and learning to be teachable.

Chapter 10: Questions for Personal Thought and Group Discussion

- What does being teachable look like for you in your life?

- What lessons has God been trying to teach you that you have resisted learning?

- What does the fact that God has unique lessons for you to learn say about His relationship to you?

- What actions in your life, what attitudes in your life, what beliefs in your life are keeping you from being teachable?

- What has God taught you in reading this book?

- What will you do about it?

ABOUT THE AUTHOR

Dr. Calvin ("Cal") Habig ministered for thirty years in Kansas, Tennessee and Oregon. In 2010 he moved into executive coaching, primarily working with clergy and non-profit executives, although he does also regularly work with business leaders. He is a 1979 graduate of Manhattan (KS) Christian College, and completed graduate work at Emmanuel School of Religion (M.Div., 1983) and Fuller Theological Seminary (D.Min., 2003). He is an ACC certified coach with the International Coach Federation and the author of three other books. He and his wife live in Portland, OR.

Cal can be followed at www.facebook.com/calhabigcoaching or at @calhabig on Twitter or at calhabigcoaching.com.

NOTES

Chapter 1

[1] teachable. (n.d.). *The American Heritage® Dictionary of the English Language, Fourth Edition*. Retrieved November 18, 2009, from Dictionary.com: http://dictionary.reference.com/browse/teachable

[2] More about the definition of "teachable" in chapter 2.

[3] Gordon McDonald, "What are the risks and rewards of being a disciple?" *Discipleship Journal, Issue 100 (July/August 1997).*

Chapter 2

[4] www.ryanbell.net

[5] Ryan J. Bell. "A Year Without God: A Former Pastor's Journey Into Atheism." Retrieved from http://www.huffingtonpost.com/ryan-j-bell/a-year-without-god_b_4512842.html.

[6] Ryan J. Bell. "A Hear Without God: A Former Pastor's Journey Into Atheism." Retrieved from http://www.patheos.com/blogs/yearwithoutgod/2013/12/31/a-year-without-god-a-former-pastors-journey-into-atheism/

[7] "Teachable" Retrieved from http://dictionary.reference.com/browse/teachable

[8] Teachable" Retrieved from http://www.thefreedictionary.com/teachable.

[9] Soanes, C., and Stevenson, A. (2004). *Concise Oxford English dictionary* (11th ed.). Oxford: Oxford University Press.

[10] Steven Covey, Principle Centered Leadership, p. 107.

[11] "Are donkeys really stubborn, asks university conference?" Retrieved from http://www.telegraph.co.uk/news/newstopics/howaboutthat/9262729/Are-donkeys-really-stubborn-asks-university-conference.html.

[12] Michael Kinsley, "The Lord and Richard Scrushy". (July 3, 2005) Retrieved from http://www.washingtonpost.com/wp-dyn/content/article/2005/07/01/AR2005070101819.html

[13] Stephen Greenspan. *The Annals of Gullibility*, p. 2.

[14] "Gullible" Retrieved from http://dictionary.reference.com/browse/gullible?s=t.

[15] Stephen Greenspan. *The Annals of Gullibility*, p. 4.

[16] Ibid.

[17] A.T. Robertson in *Word Pictures in the NT* notes on this verse: "Gullibility is no mark of a saint or of piety. Note emphatic position of you (ὑμεις [*humeis*]). Credulity ranks no higher than skepticism [sic]. God gave us our wits for self-protection. Christ has

warned us beforehand."

[18] ὁράω, εἶδον, βλέπω, ὀπτάνομαι, θεάομαι, θεωρέω. *Vol. 5: Theological dictionary of the New Testament*. 1964- (G. Kittel, G. W. Bromiley and G. Friedrich, Ed.) (electronic ed.) (p. 343). Grand Rapids, MI: Eerdmans.

[19] Vine, W. E., Unger, M. F., and White, W., Jr. (1996). *Vine's Complete Expository Dictionary of Old and New Testament Words*. Nashville, TN: T. Nelson.

[20] Christian Research Institute. *Christian Research Institute Journal Articles 2*.

[21] We don't have examples of Eve living out this lesson successfully later in life. She pretty much disappears except for child bearing after ch. 3.

[22] "Limbo Rock Lyrics" retrieved from http://www.azlyrics.com/lyrics/chubbychecker/limborock.html.

[23] Blackaby, Henry and Blackaby, Richard. *The experience*. Nashville: B and H, 1999.

Chapter 3

[24] Meyer, John D. "Stages of Learning About a Person" Retrieved from http://www.psychologytoday.com/blog/the-personality-analyst/201402/stages-learning-about-person.

[25] Bill Austin. *When God Has Put You on Hold*. Tyndale House, 1986, p. 26.

[26] Thomas Merton. *The Seven Storey Mountain*. San Diego: Harcourt Brace Javonovich, Publishers, 1948. p. 421.

[27] Morgan, R. J. (2000). *Nelson's complete book of stories, illustrations, and quotes* (electronic ed., p. 291). Nashville: Thomas Nelson Publishers.

Chapter 4

[28] Pearl S. Buck. (1947) *The Big Wave*. NY: The John Day Company. pp. 51-53.

[29] Ryken, L., Wilhoit, J., Longman, T., Duriez, C., Penney, D., and Reid, D. G. (2000). *Dictionary of biblical imagery* (electronic ed.) (591–592). Downers Grove, IL: InterVarsity Press.

[30] Harold Bullock. "Teaachableness" Audio retrieved from http://turret2.discipleshiplibrary.com/5906A.mp3.

[31] Neil Postman. (1985) *Amusing Ourselves to Death*. Penguin Books, p. 113

[32] Manser, M. H. (2009). *Dictionary of Bible Themes: The Accessible and Comprehensive Tool for Topical Studies*. London: Martin Manser.

[33] Elwell, W. A., and Beitzel, B. J. (1988). In *Baker encyclopedia of the Bible*. Grand Rapids, MI: Baker Book House.

[34] Nouwen, Henri. (1988) *Letters to Marc About Jesus*. London: Darton, Longman and Todd, p. 3-4.

[35] For any who would object that this does not apply to the teachableness of individuals since (it is argued) God treats kings and nations one way, but does not apply this principle to individuals, I would point to two New Testament examples:

Romans 1: 22-28: "Although they claimed to be wise, they became fools and exchanged the glory of the immortal God for images made to look like a mortal human being and birds and animals and reptiles. **Therefore God gave them over in the sinful desires of their hearts** to sexual impurity for the degrading of their bodies with one another.

They exchanged the truth about God for a lie, and worshiped and served created things rather than the Creator—who is forever praised. Amen. Because of this, **God gave them over to shameful lusts.** Even their women exchanged natural sexual relations for unnatural ones. In the same way the men also abandoned natural relations with women and were inflamed with lust for one another. Men committed shameful acts with other men, and received in themselves the due penalty for their error.

Furthermore, just as they did not think it worthwhile to retain the knowledge of God, **so God gave them over to a depraved mind**, so that they do what ought not to be done."

The sinfulness of individuals led to God "giving them over" to do what they had set their minds already to do. The words "God hardened their heart" are not used, but the concept is the same...the time for calling for repentance is done. The time to solidify the behavior of the disobedient is needed so that the effects of sin can be seen clearly by all.

Another example would be that of Judas Iscariot. Judas had a history of disobedience, at least, to the spirit of Christ. He criticized the sacrifice given by the woman who anointed Jesus feet with oil, and he stole from the disciples common treasury. Then in Luke 22:3 it states that *"...the chief priests and the teachers of the law were looking for some way to get rid of Jesus..... Then Satan entered Judas, called Iscariot, one of the Twelve. And Judas went to the chief priests and the officers of the temple guard and discussed with them how he might betray Jesus. They were delighted and agreed to give him money. He consented, and watched for an opportunity to hand Jesus over to them when no crowd was present.* (Luke 22:2-6)

The principle is the that God allows someone's choices to be sealed and made (at least temporarily) unchangeable, so that the person and those around him or her can see the consequences of disobedience. Or, as the text from Exodus puts it: *"so that I may perform these signs of mine among them that you may tell your children* (cont. on next page)
and grandchildren how I dealt harshly with the Egyptians and how I performed my signs among them, and that you may know that I am the LORD. (Exodus 10:1-2)."

[36] Bunyan, J. (1995). *The pilgrim's progress: From this world to that which is to come.* Oak Harbor, WA: Logos Research Systems, Inc.

[37] Nouwen (1988), p. 10.

[38] Elwell, W. A., and Beitzel, B. J. (1988). In *Baker encyclopedia of the Bible.* Grand

Rapids, MI: Baker Book House.

[39] Brian Houston. (2012) "Having a Teachable Spirit, Part 4" Retrieved from
   http://www.youtube.com/watch?v=wSezR-fXfdA

[40] *Imprimis, April 1997, Volume 26, Number 4, Hillsdale College, MI, pp. 1-2*

[41] Jones, W. (1801) *Letter 1: On a Teachable Disposition*, vol. 11, pp 209–210

[42] Jones (1801), 210.

[43] The Tortoise and the Ducks. Retrieved (and adapted) from http://www.nursery-
   rhymes-fun.com/the-tortoise-and-the-ducks.html.

Chapter 5

[44] Scotty Smith, "A Prayer for A Teachable Heart" Retrieved from
   http://thegospelcoalition.org/blogs/scottysmith/2013/08/26/a-prayer-for-a-
   teachable-heart-3/

[45] "precept" Retrieved from http://www.encyclopedia.com/topic/Precept.aspx#2.

[46] "principle" Retrieved from http://www.encyclopedia.com/topic/principle.aspx.

[47] *Reid, David. "Devotions for Growing Christians: Precept or Principles?" Retrieved from
   http://www.growingchristians.org/dfgc/precept.html.*

[48] **Almost Fifty Reason to Study and learn from God's Word from Psalm 119**

- v. 1-2-we are blessed when we allow ourselves to be taught by God's Word. (also v. 56)
- v. 4-God laid down his precepts in order that and intending that they be obeyed.
- v. 6-When we fix our eyes on His commandments, we will not be put to shame. (also v. 31)
- v. 7-learning from God's Word is a way to praise God.
- v. 9-Youth can keep his/her way pure by guarding his way according to God's Word. (i.e. allowing herself to learn from it)
- v. 11-learning from God's Word keeps you from sin. (also vv. 133)
- v. 12-God's Word teaches us:
  - ➢ 38- Hearing His promises teaches us to fear and reverence God.
  - ➢ 29- Truth and lies are made clear and separated by His Word.
  - ➢ 53-His law teaches us to see sin/sinners as He sees them.(also 136)
  - ➢ 104-His precepts teach us to hate evil and falsehood. (also 128, 163)
- v. 14-learning from God's laws brings delight (16 and 24)   and is worth the same as (or more than) great riches.
- v. 15- It gives us righteous things to meditate on.
- v. 18-There are wondrous things to behold in God's law.
- v. 19-We are visitors to this earth for a very short time. Without learning God's laws, we will not understand the world that we are passing through.
- v. 20-Our souls long for His rules and ways to be put in place in our lives.
- v. 21-Disobedience to God's laws brings rebuke.
- v. 23-When powerful people plot against us, we can rest in His Word.

- v. 24- His Word counsels us.
- v. 25-His Word brings life. (51-especially when we are afflicted)
- v. 28-Knowing God's Word gives us strength.
- v. 29-31. Being taught by God's Word is a sign of His grace. It results in keeping us from deceitful ways.
- v. 30- His Word helps us to choose rightly.
- v. 33-As we learn His Word, we learn to follow God.
- v. 36- Our hearts will turn from selfishness as we turn to His Word.
- v. 37-Our eyes will turn from worthless things as we receive life from His Word.
- v. 40-there is a connection between knowing God's precepts and God's righteousness preserving my life.
- v. 42-God's Word can be the answer for "anyone who taunts me".
- v. 43-God's promise provides comfort in suffering.
- v. 45-learning God's precepts brings freedom.
- v. 46- Knowing God's Word will help you articulate your faith.
- v. 51-God's promises bring hope when we are afflicted.
- v. 52-God's Word comforts us when we are sorrowful.
- v. 58-Indignation is a response of those who have learned from God's Word towards those who have forsaken God's law. Why?
    a. It shows disrespect to the God we love.
    b. It makes this world in which we live in more unjust and cruel because of disobedience to God's law—that results in injury to others, often innocent others.
    c. It is ultimately destructive in the life of the wicked one who has forsaken God's Law.
- v. 59-60- Meditating on God's Word motivates us to quickly obey Him!
- v. 80-Knowing God's Way produces peace in your life. (also 165)
- v. 92- If we are not delighting in His Word when trials hit, we are an easy target.
- v. 98-100- His commandments make us wise.
- v. 101- His Word reminds us to keep our feet from evil.
- v. 104-105-Knowing God's Word will guide you in making important decisions. (also v. 24, 130)
- v. 111-Knowing God's Word brings joy. (also 162)
- v. 114-His Word gives us hope and confidence each morning. (also vv.147-148)
- v. 137-His rules show us His righteousness.
- v. 140- His promises and rules are reliable, and last forever. (also 160)
- v. 155-Scripture clearly reveals the way of salvation. (v. 155).
- v. 176- Even when we go astray, His Word will be hidden in our hearts.

[49] Brinton, Henry G. "In Civil War, the Bible Became a Weapon."
"http://usatoday30.usatoday.com/news/opinion/forum/2011-02-28-

column28_ST_N.htm

Chapter 6

[50] Adapted from "The Young Crab and His Mother" Retrieved from
http://www.parenting-by-example.com/aesop-fables/THE-YOUNG-CRAB-AND-
HIS-MOTHER.pdf.

[51] When I say "stories" I am not implying that the stories are not true. In my eastern
religions class, I occasionally get Christian students who get upset when I used the
world "stories" to describe the accounts in the Bible. They see "story" as
something that is made up, fictitious, fanciful. That is not how I use the word
"story". A story is a recounting of something. Merriam-Webster's Dictionary
defines "story" as: "an account of incidents or events" ("story" retrieved from
http://www.merriam-webster.com/dictionary/story). That is how I use the word
here.

[52] "Naaman: A New Lesson Learned." *Maxwell Leadership Bible* (2002) Nashville:
Thomas Nelson Publishers. p. 454.

[53] Charles Spurgeon. (1996). Sermon: The Unchangeable Christ. In *A collection of
Sermons* (electronic ed.). Simpsonville, SC: Christian Classics Foundation, pp. 307-
326.

[54] Boles, K. L. (1993). *Galatians and Ephesians*. Joplin, MO: College Press.

Chapter 7

[55] Brian Houston. A Teachable Spirit, Part 4. Retrieved from
http://hillsongcollected.com/leadership/hillsong-tv-a-teachable-spirit-pt-4.

[56] Even though we accomplished many great things during the nine years I was at that
church and despite the effect that I was never told why I was let go, the mere fact
that it had happened puts it in the failure category. It was not a win. BUT... if
lessons can be learned from it, if I can grow from it, it can be moved closer to the
win category.

[57] John Maxwell (2000) *Failing Forward*. Nashville: Thomas Nelson, p. 13.

[58] Maxwell (2000) pp. 141-146

[59] "Discipline" Elwell, W. A., and Beitzel, B. J. (1988). In *Baker encyclopedia of the Bible*.
Grand Rapids, MI: Baker Book House.

[60] Polhill, J. B. (1995). *Acts* (Vol. 26, p. 355). Nashville: Broadman and Holman Publishers.

[61] Baptist Press. "The Lessons of Vietnam Taught Sam James to Listen, Learn" Retrieved
from http://www.bpnews.net/BPnews.asp?ID=13271.

[62] The Hebrew writer is quoting from Prov. 3.11.

[63] Ryken, L., Wilhoit, J., Longman, T., Duriez, C., Penney, D., and Reid, D. G. (2000). In
Dictionary of biblical imagery. Downers Grove, IL: InterVarsity Press.

[64] Burgo, Joseph. The Difference Between Guilt and Shame. Retrieved from

http://www.psychologytoday.com/blog/shame/201305/the-difference-between-guilt-and-shame.

[65] Efird, J. M. (2011). Shame. In (M. A. Powell, Ed.)*The HarperCollins Bible Dictionary (Revised and Updated)*. New York: HarperCollins.

Chapter 8

[66] "Principles of Learning", Retrieved from
http://dictionary.sensagent.com/Principles%20of%20learning/en-en/#Readiness.

[67] Gregory's Seven Laws are:

(1) A TEACHER must be one who KNOWS the lesson or truth or art to be taught.

(2) A LEARNER is one who ATTENDS with interest to the lesson.

(3) The LANGUAGE used as a MEDIUM between teacher and learner must be COMMON to both.

(4) The LESSON to be mastered must be explicable in the terms of truth already known by the learner--the UNKNOWN must be explained by means of the KNOWN.

(5) TEACHING is AROUSING and USING the PUPIL'S MIND to grasp the desired thought or to master the desired art.

(6) LEARNING is THINKING into one's own UNDERSTANDING a new idea or truth or working into HABIT a new art or skill.

(7) The TEST AND PROOF of teaching done--the finishing and fastening process -- must be a REVIEWING, RETHINKING, REKNOWING, REPRODUCING, and APPLYING of the material that has been taught, the knowledge and ideals and arts that have been communicated.

[68] Howard G. Hendricks. Teaching to Change Lives, p. 159.

[69] "Early School Readiness" Retrieved from
http://www.childtrends.org/?indicators=early-school-readiness

[70] Beth Lewis. "Teachable Moment." Retrieved from
http://k6educators.about.com/od/educationglossary/g/gteachmoment.htm.,

[71] John Maxwell. (2000) *Fail Forward*. Nashville: Thomas Nelson Publishers, p. 13.

[72] Pain and Pleasure. Retrieved from http://www.secularcafe.org/archive/index.php/t-13320.html.

[73] C.R. Chapman. Why Does Pain Hurt. Retrieved from http://www.project-syndicate.org/commentary/why-does-pain-hurt.

[74] Maxwell (2000), p.217

[75] Chesterton,G.K. (1993) Collected Works: Vol. 14: Short Stories, Fairy Tales, Mystery Stories--Illustrations. Edited by Denis J. Conlon. Ignatius Press. p. 350.

[76] Thomas Merton. (n.d.). BrainyQuote.com. Retrieved from
http://www.brainyquote.com/quotes/quotes/t/thomasmert390404.html

[77] Andrew Murray. (n.d.) *Abide in Christ*. Philadelphia: Henry Altimus Company, p. 1

78 "Chastisement, Chasten" in Elwell, W. A., and Beitzel, B. J. (1988).*Baker encyclopedia of the Bible*. Grand Rapids, MI: Baker Book House.

79 e.g. Proverbs 3:11: My son, do not despise the LORD's discipline, and do not resent his rebuke, because the LORD disciplines those he loves, as a father the son he delights in.
Psalm 94:12: Blessed is the one you discipline, LORD, the one you teach from your law;
Psalm 94:10: Does he who disciplines nations not punish? Does he who teaches mankind lack knowledge?

80 F.B. Meyer. *The Way into the Holiest: Expositions of the Book of Hebrews*. Grand Rapids: Baker Book House, 1951., n.p.

81 William Saroyan. *My Heart is in the Highlands*. Samuel French, Inc. (1968)

82 Timothy Gallwey. *The Inner Game of Tennis*. Random House Publishers, 1974. p. 18

83 Timothy Gallwey. *The Inner Game of Tennis*. Random House Publishers, 1974. p. 37.

84 Timothy Gallwey, "Inner Game Headlines, News and Events" Retrieved from www.theinnergame.com.

85 "Natural Stuff" Retrieved from http://www.totallyuselessknowledge.com/natural.php

86 Maxwell, John. Failing Forward. Nashville: Thomas Nelson, 2000, p. 145-146.

87 Spurgeon, C. H. (1995). *2,200 quotations: from the writings of Charles H. Spurgeon : arranged topically or textually and indexed by subject, Scripture, and people*. (T. Carter, Ed.) (p. 158). Grand Rapids, MI: Baker Books.

88 Gregory, John Milton. *The 7 Laws of Teaching*. Grand Rapids, MI: Baker Book House, 1917 revised edition, p. 29.

Chapter 9

89 "Talkative pastor finds a teachable moment" Retrieved from http://www.thechaplain.net/Articles.aspx?id=3117405.

90 Aaron Story. "Teachability." Retrieved from http://aaronstory.com/leadership-blog/the-unteachable-leader/)

91 I have used this passage several times in this book, but I unashamedly use it again!

92 αυθαδησ; ESV, NRSV, TEV-"arrogant"; KJV, NASB, ASV and Amplified-"self-willed"; New Century-"selfish"; God's Word-"stubborn"

93 *International standard version New Testament: Version 1.1*. 2000 (Print on Demand ed.) (2 Ti 2:24). Yorba Linda, CA: The Learning Foundation.

94 Cyprian of Carthage. (1886). The Epistles of Cyprian. In A. Roberts, J. Donaldson, & A. C. Coxe (Eds.), R. E. Wallis (Trans.), *Fathers of the Third Century: Hippolytus, Cyprian, Novatian, Appendix* (Vol. 5). Buffalo, NY: Christian Literature Company.p. 338.

95 Augustine of Hippo. (1887). On Baptism, against the Donatists. In P. Schaff (Ed.), J. R. King (Trans.), *St. Augustin: The Writings against the Manichaeans and against the Donatists* (Vol. 4). Buffalo, NY: Christian Literature Company.

96 Emphasis mine.

[97] Eli Cohen and Noel Tichy. *How Leaders Develop Leaders. Training and Development*, May, 1997, p. 5.

[98] Amy K. Donahue and Robert V. Tuohy. "Lessons We Don't Learn: A Study of the Lessons of Disasters, Why We Repeat Them, and How We Can Learn Them" Homeland Security Affairs, Vol II,No. 2 (July 2006), p. 7.

[99] Matthew who was writing primarily to Jews only identifies her as "a Canaanite" (because that was known by the Jews as the former region of Canaan), but Mark specifically tells where she was from--"Syrophoenicia"-- since he was writing primarily to Greek speakers and they would be more familiar with the political designation of the Phoenician area [the area around the city of Tyre] of the Roman province of Syria.

[100] John E. Michel. "For The Weary Leader." Retrieved from http://switchandshift.com/for-the-weary-leader.

[101] Laughing Conservative. "Condoleezza: 'leaders can't afford to be weary'." Retrieved from http://laughingconservative.blogspot.com/2014/03/condoleezza-leaders-cat-afford-to-be.html.

[102] Orr, J. (n.d.). *The International Standard Bible Encyclopedia* (electronic ed.).

[103] "Statler Brothers—Fourth Man Lyrics retrieved from http://artists.letssingit.com/statler-brothers-lyrics-the-fourth-man-3z8kkmf

[104] http://www.paulchappell.com/2009/09/28/20-characteristics-of-a-christ-like-leader/

[105] Michael Molloy, *Experiencing the World's Religions*. McGraw-Hi, 2013, p. 103.

[106] "What is Groupthink?" Retrieved from http://psychology.about.com/od/gindex/g/groupthink.htm.

[107] Irving Janis, *Victims of Groupthink*, Houghton Mifflin, Boston, 1972, p. 9.

[108] "Teachability: If We Don't Learn from History, We Will Repeat it". *The Leadership Bible*. Thomas Nelson, 2002, p. 1125.

Chapter 10

(none)

Made in the USA
Charleston, SC
16 January 2015